GUIDE TO THE SAVIOR.

GUIDE

TO

THE SAVIOR.

OR

Conditions of Attaining to and Abiding in

ENTIRE HOLINESS OF HEART AND LIFE.

BY PROF. C. G. FINNEY.

THIRD EDITION.

OBERLIN:

JAMES M. FITCH.

1855.

Entered according to act of Congress, in the year 1848, by

CHARLES G. FINNEY,

In the Clerk's office of the District Court of Ohio.

INTRODUCTION.

THIS little volume contains six lectures, making a part of my course of lectures on entire sanctification in this life, as published in the third volume of my Systematic Theology. I have been repeatedly urged to consent to the publication of these lectures in a small volume by themselves, for the following reasons:

1. Their value to many Christians who can not afford to purchase the entire work on Systematic Theology.

2. Their value to those who, though able to purchase the entire work, have not sufficient leisure to read it.

3. Their value to young Christians and to all that class of persons who would not be able to read and comprehend the larger work entire.

4. They are thought to contain that spiritual food which is greatly needed by all classes of Christians, and should, therefore, as far as possible, be put within the reach of all, and in a form and size the least expensive and most convenient.

Let it be borne in mind that these six lectures are confined to a presentation of the *conditions of abiding holiness* of heart and life. They are designed, *not* to define entire sanctification, *not* to prove its attainability—nor that it has been attained, but simply to indicate the necessary *conditions* or *means of continuing* in obedience to God. Those who would understand my views of the whole subject, must read and *ponder well* the entire course of lectures upon the subject, as found in the third volume to the first edition of my Systematic Theology.

The full scope and bearing of these six lectures will not be so fully seen, separated from the entire course, but it is thought that by themselves they contain sufficient spiritual instruction to warrant and demand a separate publication.

I might, as is indicated in the lectures themselves,

greatly enlarge every head, and swell this to a large volume. But, first, I have not time to do so. Secondly, the volume would then be too large for multitudes of purchasers and readers. Thirdly, on many of the relations of Christ to believers, I greatly desire to enlarge, but upon the whole, I will consent to have the lectures presented as they are found in the original work.

To Christ and his dear children I consecrate these lectures. If any one shall be refreshed by their perusal, I shall be happy to give *all the glory to Christ*, and be content myself with the satisfaction of having been made instrumental in feeding the "flock of God which he has purchased with his own blood."

THE AUTHOR.

CONTENTS.

1*

CHAPTER II.

CONDITIONS OF ATTAINING TO HOLINESS, CONTINUED.

CHAPTER VI.

CONDITIONS OF ATTAINING TO HOLINESS, CONTINUED.

GUIDE TO THE SAVIOR.

CHAPTER I.

CONDITIONS OF ATTAINING TO HOLINESS.

I. A state of entire sanctification can never be attained by an indifferent waiting of God's time.

II. Nor by any works of law, or works of any kind performed in your own strength, irrespective of the grace of God. By this I do not mean that, were you disposed to exert your natural powers aright, you could not at once obey the law in the exercise of your natural strength and continue to do so. But I do mean, that as you are wholly indisposed to use your natural powers aright without the grace of God, no efforts that you will actually make in your own strength or independent of his grace, will ever result in your entire sanctification.

III. Not by any direct efforts to feel right. Many spend their time in vain efforts to force themselves into a right state of feeling. Now it should be forever understood, that religion does not consist in a mere feeling, emotion, or involuntary affection of any kind. Feelings do not result from a direct effort to feel. But on the contrary, they are the spontaneous actings of the mind when it has under its direct and deep consideration the objects, truths, facts or realities that are correlated to these involuntary emotions. They are the most easy and natural state of mind possible under such circumstances. So far from its requiring an effort to put them forth, it would rather require an effort to prevent them, when the mind is intensely considering those objects and considerations which have a natural tendency to produce them. This is so true that when persons are in the exercise of such affections, they feel no difficulty at all in their exercise, but wonder how any one can help feeling as they do. It seems to them so natural, so easy, and I may say so almost unavoidable, that they often feel and express astonishment that any one should find it difficult to exercise the feelings of which they are conscious. The course that many persons take on the subject of religion has often appeared wonderful to me. They make themselves, their own state and interest, the central point around which their own minds are continually revolving. Their selfishness is so great that their own interests, happiness, and salvation, fill their whole field of vision. And with their thoughts and anxieties, and whole souls clustering around their own salvation, they complain of a hard heart—that they can not love God—that they do not repent and can not believe. They manifestly regard love to God, repentance, faith, and all religion, as consisting in *mere feeling*. Being conscious that they do not *feel* right, as they express it, they are the more concerned about themselves, which concern but increases their embarassment and the difficulty of exercising what they call right affections. The less they feel, the more they try to feel—the greater efforts they make to feel right without success, the more are they confirmed in their selfishness, and the more are their thoughts glued to their own interests; and they are of course at a greater and greater distance from any right state of mind. And thus their selfish anxieties beget ineffectual efforts, and these efforts but deepen their anxieties. And if in this state, death should appear in a visible form before them, or the last trumpet sound, and they should be sum-

moned to the solemn Judgment it would
but increase their distraction, confirm and
almost give omnipotence to their selfishness, and render their sanctification
morally impossible. It should never be
forgotten that all true religion consists in
voluntary states of mind, and that the
true and only way to attain to true religion is to look at and understand the ex-
act thing to be done and then to put forth
at once the voluntary exercise required.

IV. Not by any efforts to obtain grace
by works of law. In my lecture on
Faith, in the first volume of the Evange-
list, I said the following things:

1. Should the Question be proposed to
a Jew, " What shall I do that I may work
the works of God ?"—he would answer,
Keep the law, both moral and ceremonial,
that is, keep the commandments.

2. To the same inquiry an Arminian
would answer, Improve common grace,
and you will obtain converting grace,
that is, use the means of grace according

to the best light you have, and you will
obtain the grace of salvation. In this
answer it is not supposed, that the inquirer already has faith; but that he is in a
state of unbelief, and is inquiring after
converting grace. The answer, therefore, amounts to this; you must get converting grace by your *impenitent* works ;
you must become holy by your hypocri-
sy ; you must work out sanctification by
sin.

3. To this question, most professed Cal-
vinists would make in substance the same
reply. They would reject the language
while they retain the idea. Their direction would imply, either that the inquirer
already has faith, or that he must perform
some works to obtain it, that is, that he
must obtain grace by works of law.

A late Calvinistic writer admits that
entire and permanent sanctification is at-
tainable, although he rejects the idea of
the actual attainment of such a state in
this life. He supposes the condition of

attaining this state or the way to attain
it, is by a diligent use of the means of
grace and that the saints are sanctified
just so far as they make a diligent use of
the means of sanctification. But as he
denies that any saints ever did or will use
all the means with suitable diligence, he
denies also of course that entire sanctification ever is attained in this life. The
way of attaining it, according to his
teaching, is by the diligent use of means.
If then this writer were asked, "What
shall I do to work the works of God,"—
or in other words, what shall I do to obtain entire and permanent sanctification,
his answer, it seems, would be : "Use dili-
gently all the means of grace," that is,
you must get grace by works, or, with the
Arminian, improve common grace and
you will secure sanctifying grace.

Neither an Arminian, nor a Calvinist,
would *formally* direct the inquirer to the
law, as the ground of Justification. But
nearly the whole Church would give di-

rections that would amount to the same thing. Their answer would be a legal, and not a gospel answer. For whatever answer is given to this question, that does not distinctly recognize *faith*, as the condition of abiding holiness in Christians, is legal. Unless the inquirer is made to understand, that this is the first, grand, fundamental duty, without the performance of which all virtue, all giving up of sin, all acceptable obedience, is impossible, he is misdirected. He is led to believe that it is possible to please God without faith, and to obtain grace by works of law. There are but two kinds of works—works of law, and works of faith. Now if the inquirer has not the "faith which works by love," to set him upon any course of works to get it, is certainly to set him to get faith by works of law. Whatever is said to him that does not clearly convey the truth, that both justification and sanctification are by faith, without works of law, is law and not gospel. Nothing before or without faith, can possibly be done by any one, but works of law. His first duty, therefore, is faith; and every attempt to obtain faith by unbelieving works, is to lay works at the foundation, and make grace a result. It is the direct opposite of gospel truth.

Take facts as they arise in every day's experience, to show that what I have stated is true of almost all professors and non-professors. Whenever a sinner begins in good earnest to agitate the question, " What shall I do to be saved?" he resolves as a first duty to break off from his sins, that is, in unbelief. Of course, his reformation is only outward. He determines to do better—to reform in this, that, and the other thing, and thus prepare himself to be converted. He does not expect to be saved without grace and faith but he attempts to get grace by works of law.

The same is true of multitudes of anxious Christians, who are inquiring what they shall do to overcome the world, the flesh, and the devil. They overlook the fact, that " this is the victory which over- cometh the world, even our faith," that it is with " the shield of faith " that they are " to quench all the fiery darts of the wick- ed." They ask, Why am I overcome by sin? Why can I not get above its power? Why am I thus the slave of my appetites and passions, and the sport of the devil? They cast about for the cause of all this spiritual wretchedness and death. At one time, they think they have discovered it in the neglect of one duty; and at anoth- er time in the neglect of another. Some- times they imagine they have found the cause to lie in yielding to one sin, and sometimes in yielding to another. They put forth efforts in this direction, and in that direction, and patch up their right- eousness on one side, while they make a rent on the other side. Thus they spend years in running around in a circle, and making dams of sand across the current of their own habitudes and tendencies.

Instead of at once *purifying their hearts
by faith,* they are engaged in trying to
arrest the overflowing of the bitter waters of their own propensities. *Why* do
I sin? they inquire; and casting about for
the cause, they come to the sage conclusion, It is because I neglect such a duty,
that is, because I do sin. But how shall
I get rid of sin? Answer: by doing my
duty, that is, by ceasing from sin. Now
the real inquiry is, *Why* do they neglect
their duty? Why do they commit sin at
all? Where is the foundation of all this
mischief? Will it be replied, the foundation of all this wickedness is in the force
of temptation—in the weakness of our
hearts—in the strength of our evil propensities and habits? But all this only
brings us back to the real inquiry again,
how are these things to be overcome? I
answer, by faith alone. No works of
law have the least tendency to overcome
our sins; but rather to confirm the soul
in self-righteousness and unbelief.

The great and fundamental sin, which is at the foundation of all other sin, is unbelief. The first thing is to give up that—to believe the word of God. There is no breaking off from one sin without this. " Whatsoever is not of faith is sin." " Without faith it is impossible to please God."

Thus we see that the backslider and convicted sinner, when agonizing to overcome sin, will almost always betake themselves to works of law to obtain faith. They will fast, and pray, and read, and struggle, and outwardly reform, and thus endeavor to obtain grace. Now all this is in vain and wrong. Do you ask, shall we not fast, and pray, and read, and struggle? Shall we do nothing—but sit down in Antinomian security and inaction? I answer, You must do all that God commands you to do: but begin where He tells you to begin, and do it in the manner in which He commands you to do it ; that is, in the exercise of that faith that works by love. Purify your hearts by faith. Believe in the Son of God. And say not in your heart, " Who shall ascend into heaven, that is, to bring Christ down from above; or who shall descend into the deep, that is, to bring up Christ again from the dead. But what saith it? The word is nigh thee, even in thy mouth and in thy heart, that is, the word of faith which we preach."

Now these facts show that even under the gospel, many professors of religion, while they reject the Jewish notion of justification by works of law, have, after all, adopted a ruinous substitute for it, and suppose that, in some way they are to *obtain grace by their works.*

V. A state of entire sanctification cannot be attained by attempting to copy the experience of others. It is very common for convicted sinners, or for Christians inquiring after entire sanctification, in their blindness, to ask others to relate their experience, to mark minutely the detail

2

of all their exercises, and then set themselves to pray for and make direct efforts to attain the same class of exercises—not seeming to understand that they can no more exercise feelings in the detail like others, than they can look like others. Human experiences differ as human countenances differ. The whole history of a man's former state of mind, comes in of course to modify his present and future experience. So that the precise train of feelings which may be requisite in your case, and which will actually occur, if you are ever sanctified, will not in all its details, coincide with the exercises of any other human being. It is of vast importance for you to understand, that you can be no copyist in any true religious experience: and that you are in great danger of being deceived by Satan whenever you attempt to copy the experience of others. I beseech you, therefore, to cease from praying for or trying to obtain the precise experience of any person whatever. All truly

Christian experiences, are, like human countenances, in their outline, so much alike, as to be readily known as the lineaments of the religion of Jesus Christ. But no farther than this are they alike, any more than human countenances are alike.

But here let it be remembered that sanctification does not consist in the various affections or emotions of which Christians speak, and which are often mistaken for or confounded with true religion; but that sanctification consists in entire consecration, and consequently it is all out of place for any one to attempt to copy the feelings of another, inasmuch as feelings do not constitute religion. The feelings of which Christians speak do not constitute true religion, but often result from a right state of heart. These feelings may properly enough be spoken of as Christian experience, for, although involuntary states of mind, they are experienced by true Christians. The only way to secure them is to set the will right, and the emotions will be a natural result.

VI. Not by waiting to make preparations before you come into this state. Observe that the thing about which you are inquiring is a state of entire consecration to God. Now do not imagine that this state of mind must be prefaced by a long introduction of preparatory exercises. It is common for persons when inquiring upon this subject with earnestness, to think themselves hindered in their progress by a want of this or that or the other exercise or state of mind. They look every where else but at the real difficulty. They assign any other and every other but the true reason for their not being already in a state of sanctification. The true difficulty is voluntary selfishness or voluntary consecration to self-interest and self-gratification. This is the difficulty and the only difficulty to be overcome.

VII. Not by attending meetings, asking the prayers of other Christians, or depending in any way upon the means of getting into this state. By this I do not intend to say that means are unnecessary, or that it is not through the instrumentality of truth, that this state of mind is induced. But I do mean that while you are depending upon any instrumentality whatever, your mind is diverted from the real point before you, and you are never like to make this attainment.

VIII. Not by waiting for any particular views of Christ. When persons, in the state of mind of which I have been speaking, hear those who live in faith describe their views of Christ, they say, O, if I had such *views*, I could believe ; I must have these before I can believe. Now you should understand that these *views* are the result and effect of faith in the promise of the Spirit to take of the things of Christ and show them to you. Lay hold of this class of promises, and the Holy Spirit will reveal Christ to you in the relations in which you need Him from time to time. Take hold, then, on the simple promise of God. Take God at his word. Believe that He means just what He says; and this will at once bring you into the state of mind after which you inquire.

IX. Not in any way which you may mark out for yourself. Persons in an inquiring state are very apt, without seeming to be aware of it, to send imagination on before them, to stake out the way, and set up a flag where they intend to come out. They expect to be thus and thus exercised—to have such and such peculiar views and feelings, when they have attained their object. Now there probably never was a person who did not find himself disappointed in these respects. God says, " I will bring the blind by a way that they know not. I will lead them in paths that they have not known: I will make darkness light before them, and crooked things straight. These things will I do unto them, and not forsake them." This suffering your imagination to mark out your path is a great hindrance to you, as it sets you upon making many fruitless and worse than fruitless, attempts to attain this imaginary state of mind, wastes much of your time, and greatly wearies the patience and grieves the Spirit of God. While He is trying to lead you right to the point, you are hauling off from the course, and insisting that this which your imagination has marked out is the way, instead of that in which He is trying to lead you. And thus in your pride and ignorance you are causing much delay, and abusing the long-suffering of God. He says, "This is the way, walk ye in it." But you say, no—*this* is the way. And thus you stand and parley and banter, while you are every moment in danger of grieving the Spirit of God away from you and of losing your soul.

X. Not in any manner, or at any time nor place, upon which you may in your own mind lay any stress. If there is any thing in your imagination that has fixed definitely upon any particular manner, time, or place, or circumstance, you will in all probability either be deceived by the devil, or be entirely disappointed in the result. You will find that in all these particular items on which you had laid any stress, that the wisdom of man is foolishness with God—that your ways are not his ways, nor your thoughts his thoughts. " For as the heavens are higher than the earth, so are his ways higher than your ways, and his thoughts higher than your thoughts."

But,

XI. This state is to be attained by faith alone. Let it be forever remembered, that " without faith it is impossible to please God," and " whatsoever is not of faith, is sin."

Both justification and sanctification are by faith alone. Rom. 3: 30; " Seeing it is one God who shall justify the circumcision by faith, and the uncircumcision through faith ;" and 5: 1; " Therefore, being justified by faith, we have peace with God through our Lord Jesus Christ." Also, 9: 30, 31 ; "What shall we say then ? that the Gentiles, who followed not after righteousness, have attained to righteousness, even the righteousness which is of faith. But Israel, who followed after the law of righteousness, hath *not* attained to the law of righteousness. Wherefore? Because they sought it not by faith, but, as it were, by the works of the law."

XII. But let me by no means be understood as teaching sanctification by faith as distinct from and opposed to sanctification by the Holy Spirit or Spirit of Christ, or, which is the same thing, by Christ our sanctification living and reigning in the heart. Faith is rather the instrument or condition than the efficient agent that induces a state of present and permanent sanctification. Faith, simply receives Christ, as king, to live and reign in the soul. It is Christ in the exercise of his different offices and appropriated in his

2*

different relations to the wants of the soul, by faith, who secures our sanctification. This he does by divine discoveries to the soul of his Divine perfections and fullness. The condition of these discoveries is faith and obedience. He says, Jno. 14: 21—23—"He that hath my commandments, and keepeth them, he it is that loveth me; and he that loveth me shall be loved of my Father, and I will love him, and will manifest myself to him. Judas saith unto Him, (not Iscariot,) Lord, how is it that thou wilt manifest thyself unto us, and not unto the world? Jesus answered and said unto him, If a man love me, he will keep my words: and my Father will love him, and we will come unto him, and make our abode with him." But I must call your attention to Christ as our sanctification more at large hereafter.

CHAPTER II.

To ascertain the conditions of entire sanctification in this life we need to consider what the temptations are that overcome us. When first converted we have seen that the heart or will consecrates itself and the whole being to God. We have also seen that this is a state of disinterested benevolence or a committal of the whole being to the promotion of the highest good of being. We have also seen that all sin is selfishness, or that all sin consists in the will's seeking the indulgence or gratification of self; that it consists in the will's yielding obedience to the propensities, instead of obeying God, as his law is revealed in the reason. Now

who can not see what needs to be done
to break the power of temptation and let
the soul go free? The fact is that the department of our sensibility as related to
objects of time and sense, has received an
enormous development and is tremblingly
alive to all its correlated objects, while
by reason of the blindness of the mind to
spiritual objects, it is scarcely developed
at all in its relations to them. Those objects are seldom thought of by the carnal
mind, and when they are they are only
thought of. They are not clearly seen,
and of course they are not felt.

The thought of God, of Christ, of sin, of
holiness, of heaven, and hell, excites little
or no emotion in the carnal mind. The
carnal mind is alive and awake to earthly
and sensible objects, but dead to spiritual
realities. The spiritual world needs to be
revealed to the soul. The soul needs to
see and clearly apprehend its own spiritual condition, relations, wants. It needs
to become acquainted with God and Christ,

to have spiritual and eternal realities made plain, and present, and all-absorbing realities to the soul. It needs such discoveries of the eternal world, of the nature and guilt of sin, and of Christ, the Remedy of the soul, as to kill or greatly mortify lust, or the appetites and passions in their relations to objects of time and sense, and to thoroughly develop the sensibility in its relations to sin and to God, and to the whole circle of spiritual realities. This will greatly abate the frequency and power of temptation to self-gratification, and break up the voluntary slavery of the will. The developments of the sensibility need to be thoroughly corrected. This can only be done by the revelation by the Holy Spirit, to the inward man, of those great and solemn and overpowering realities of the " spirit land," that lie concealed from the eye of flesh.

We often see those around us whose sensibility is so developed in some one or more directions, that they are led captive by appetite and passion in that direction in spite of reason and of God. The inebriate is an example of this. The glutton, the licentious, the avaricious man, &c., are examples of this kind. We sometimes, on the other hand, see by some striking providence such a counter development of the sensibility produced as to slay and put down those particular tendencies, and the whole direction of the man's life seems to be changed; and outwardly, at least, it is so. From being a perfect slave to his appetite for strong drink, he can not without the utmost loathing and disgust so much as hear the name of his once loved beverage mentioned. From being a most avaricious man be becomes deeply disgusted with wealth, and spurns and despises it. Now this has been effected by a counter development of the sensibility, for in the case supposed religion has nothing to do with it. Religion does not consist in the states of the sensibility, nor in the will's being influenced by sensibility; but *sin* consists in the will's being thus influenced. One great thing that needs to be done to confirm and settle the will in the attitude of entire consecration to God, is to bring about a counter development of the sensibility, so that it will not draw the will away from God. It needs to be mortified or crucified to the world, to objects of time and sense, by so deep, and clear, and powerful a revelation of self to self, and of Christ to the soul as to awaken and develop all its susceptibilities in their relations to him and to spiritual and divine realities. This can easily be done through and by the Holy Spirit, who takes of the things of Christ, and shows them to us. He so reveals Christ that the soul receives him to the throne of the heart and to reign throughout the whole being. When the will, the intellect, and the sensibility are yielded to him, he develops the intelligence and the sensibility by clear revelations of himself in all his offices and relations to the soul, confirms the will, mellows and chastens the sensibility by these divine revelations to the intelligence.

FIRST. It is plain that men are naturally able to be entirely sanctified in the sense of rendering entire and continual obedience to God; for the ability is the condition of the obligation to do so. But what is implied in ability to be holy as God requires us to be?

The ready and plain answer to this question is:

1. The possession of the powers and susceptibilities of moral agents. 2. Sufficient knowledge or light to reveal to us the whole of duty. 3. And also to reveal to us clearly the way and means of overcoming any and every difficulty or temptation that lies in our way.

The first we all possess. The second we also possess, for nothing strictly is or can be duty that is not revealed or made known to us. The third is proffered to us upon condition that we receive the

Holy Spirit who offers himself as an indwelling light and guide, and who is received by simple faith.

The light and grace which we need and which it is the office of the Holy Spirit to supply, respects mainly the following things :

FIRST. Knowledge of ourselves, our past sins, their nature, aggravation, guilt and desert of dire damnation.

SECOND. Knowledge of our spiritual helplessness or weakness in consequence of

1. The physical depravity of our natures. 2. Of the strength of selfish habit. 3. Because of the power of temptation from the world, the flesh, and Satan.

THIRD. We need the light of the Holy Spirit to teach us the character of God, the nature of his government, the purity of his law, the necessity and fact of atonement.

FOURTH. To teach us our need of Christ in all his offices and relations, governmental, spiritual, and mixed.

FIFTH. If we would be led fully to the Savior, we need a revelation of him to our souls in such power as to induce in us that appropriating faith without which he is not and cannot be our salvation.

SIXTH. We need to know him in such relations as the following;

I. As King, to set up his government and write his law in our hearts; to establish his kingdom within us; to sway his sceptre over our whole being. As king he must be spiritually revealed and received.

II. As our Mediator, to stand between the offended justice of God and our guilty souls, to bring about a reconciliation between our souls and God. As Mediator he must be known and received.

III. As our Advocate, or *Paracletos*, our next or best friend, to plead our cause with the Father, our righteous and all-pervading Advocate to secure the triumph of our cause at the bar of God. In this relation he must be apprehended and embraced.

IV. As our Redeemer, to redeem us from the curse of the law and from the power and dominion of sin; to pay the price demanded by public justice for our release, and to overcome and break up forever our spiritual bondage. In this relation also we must know and appreciate him by faith.

V. As our Justification, to procure our pardon and acceptance with God. To know him and embrace him in this relation is indispensable to peace of mind and to release from the condemnation of the law.

VI. As our Judge, to pronounce sentence of acceptance, and to award to us the victor's crown.

VII. As the Repairer of the Breach, or as the one who makes good to the government of God our default, or in other words, who, by his obedience unto death, rendered to the public justice of

God a full governmental equivalent for
the infliction of the penalty of the law
upon us.

VIII. As the propitiation for our sins,
to offer himself as a *propitiatory*, or offering for our sins. The apprehension of
Christ as making an atonement for our
sins seems to- be indispensable to the en-
tertaining of a healthy hope of eternal
life.   It certainly is not healthy for the
soul to apprehend the mercy of God
without regarding the conditions of its
exercise.   It does not sufficiently impress
the soul with the sense of the justice and
holiness of God, with the guilt and desert
of sin.   It does not sufficiently awe the
soul and humble it in the deepest dust to
regard God as extending pardon without
regard to the sternness of his justice, as
evinced in requiring that sin should be recognized in the universe as worthy of the
wrath and curse of God, as a condition of
its forgiveness.   It is remarkable and well
worthy of all consideration that those who

deny the atonement make sin a compara-
tive trifle, and seem to regard God's benevolence or love as good nature rather
than, as it is, "a consuming fire" to all the
workers of iniquity. Nothing does or can
produce that awe of God, that fear and
holy dread of sin, that sense of self-abase-
ment, that self-abasing, God-justifying
spirit, that a thorough apprehension of
the atonement of Christ will do. Nothing
like this can beget that spirit of self-renunciation, of cleaving to Christ, of taking refuge in his blood. In these relations Christ
must be revealed to and apprehended and
embraced by us as the condition of our
entire sanctification.

IX. As a surety of a better than the
first covenant, that is, as a surety of a
gracious covenant founded on better
promises; as an underwriter or endorsor
of our obligation; as one who undertakes
for us and pledges himself as our security
to fulfill for and in us all the conditions of
our salvation. To apprehend and appro-

priate Christ by faith in this relation is no doubt a condition of our entire sanctification. I should greatly delight to enlarge and write a whole course of lectures on the offices and relations of Christ, the necessity of knowing and appropriating him in these relations as the condition of our entire, in the sense of continued sanctication. This would require a large volume at least. All that I can do is to merely suggest a skeleton outline of this subject in its place.

X. We need to apprehend and appropriate Christ as dying for *our* sins. It is the work of the Holy Spirit to thus reveal his death in its relations to our *individual sins,* and as related to *our* sins as individuals. The soul needs to apprehend Christ as *crucified for us.* It is one thing for the soul to regard the death of Christ merely as the death of a martyr, and an infinitely different thing, as every one knows who has had the experience, to apprehend his death as a real and veritable vicarious sacrifice for our sins, as being truly a substitute for our death. The soul needs to apprehend Christ as suffering on the cross for *it*, or as its substitute; so that it can say, that sacrifice is for me, that suffering and that death are for *my* sins. That blessed Lamb is slain for my sins. If thus fully to apprehend and to appropriate Christ, can not kill sin in us, what can?

XL. We need also to know Christ as *risen for our justification*. He arose and lives to procure our certain acquittal or our complete pardon and acceptance with God. That he lives, and is our justification, we need to know, to break the bondage of legal motives and to slay all selfish fear; to break and destroy the power of temptation from this source. The clearly, convinced soul is often tempted to despondency and unbelief, to despair of its own acceptance with God, and it would surely fall into the bondage of fear, were it not for the faith of Christ as a risen, living, justifying Savior. In this relation the soul needs clearly to apprehend and fully to appropriate Christ in his completeness, as a condition of abiding in a state of disinterested consecration to God.

XII. We need also to have Christ revealed to us as bearing our griefs and as carrying our sorrows. The clear apprehension of Christ as being made sorrowful for us, and as bending under sorrows and griefs that in justice belonged to us, tends at once to render sin unspeakably odious and Christ infinitely precious to our souls. The idea of Christ our substitute needs to be thoroughly developed in our minds. And this relation of Christ needs to be so clearly revealed to us as to become an every where present reality to us. We need to have Christ so revealed as to so completely ravish and engross our affections that we would sooner cut our own throats or suffer others to cut them, than to sin against him. Is such a thing impossible? Indeed it is not. Is not the Holy Spirit able, and willing, and ready to thus reveal him upon condition of our asking it in faith? Surely he is.

XIII. We also need to apprehend Christ as the one by whose stripes we are healed. We need to know him as relieving our pains and sufferings by his own, as preventing our death by his own, as sorrowing that we might eternally rejoice, as grieving that we might be unspeakably and eternally glad, as dying in unspeakable agony that we might die in deep peace and in unspeakable triumph.

XIV. *"As being made sin for us."* We need to apprehend him as being treated as a sinner, and even as the chief of sinners, on our account, or for us. This is the representation of scripture, that Christ on our account was treated as if he were a sinner. He was made sin for us, that is, he was treated as a sinner, or rather as being the representative, or as it were the embodiment of sin for us. Of this the soul needs to apprehend—the holy Jesus treated as a sinner, and as if

3

all sin were consecrated in him, on our
account! We procured this treatment of
him. He consented to take our place in
such a sense as to endure the cross, and
the curse of the law for us. When the
soul apprehends this, it is ready to die
with grief and love. O, how infinitely it
loathes itself under such an apprehension
as this! In this relation he must not only
be apprehended, but appropriated by
faith.

XV. We need also to apprehend the
fact that *"He was made sin for us that we
might be made the righteousness of God
in him ;"* that Christ was treated as a
sinner that we might be treated as righteous; that we might also be made personally righteous by faith in him; that we
might be made the *righteousness of God
in him;* that we might inherit and be
made partakers of God's righteousness as
that righteousness exists and is revealed
in Christ; that we might in and by him
be made righteous as God is righteous.

The soul needs to see that his being made sin for us, was in order that we might be made the righteousness of God in him. It needs to embrace and lay hold by faith upon that righteousness of God which is brought home to saints in Christ through the atonement and indwelling Spirit.

XVI. We also need him revealed to the soul as one upon whose shoulders is the government of the world; who administers the government moral and providential of this world for the protection, discipline and benefit of believers. This revelation has a most sin-subduing tendency. That all events are directly or indirectly controlled by Him who has so loved us as to die for us; that all things absolutely are designed for and will surely result in our good—these and such like considerations when revealed to the soul and made living realities to the Holy Spirit tend to kill selfishness and confirm the love of God in the soul.

. XVII. We also need Christ revealed to the inward being as *Head over all things to the church*. All these relations are of no avail to our sanctification only in so far forth as they are directly and inwardly and personally revealed to the soul by the Holy Spirit. It is one thing to have thoughts and ideas and opinions concerning Christ, and an entirely different thing to know Christ as he is revealed by the Holy Spirit. All the relations of Christ imply corresponding necessities in us. When the Holy Spirit has revealed to us the necessity and Christ as exactly suited to fully meet that necessity, and urged his acceptance in that relation until we have appropriated him by faith, a great work is done. But until we are thus revealed to ourselves and Christ is thus revealed to us and accepted by us, nothing is done more than to store our heads with notions or opinions and theories, while our hearts are becoming more and more, at every moment, like an adamant stone.

I have often feared that many professed Christians knew Christ only after the flesh, that is, they have no other knowledge of Christ than what they obtain by reading and hearing about him without any special revelation of him to the inward being by the Holy Spirit. I do not wonder that such professors and ministers should be totally in the dark upon the subject of entire sanctification in this life. They regard sanctification as brought about by the formation of holy habits instead of resulting from the revelation of Christ to the soul in all his fullness and relations, and the soul's renunciation of self and appropriation of Christ in all these relations. Christ is represented in the Bible as the Head of the church. The church is represented as his body. He is to the church what the head is to the body. The head is the seat of intelligence, the will, and in short of the living soul. Consider what the body would be without the head, and you may under-

stand what the church would be without
Christ.   But as the church would be
without Christ, so each believer would
be without Christ.   But we need to have
our necessities in this respect clearly revealed to us by the Holy Spirit, and this
relation of Christ made plain to our
apprehension. The utter darkness of the
human mind in regard to its own spiritual
state and wants, and in regard to the
relations and fullness of Christ is truly
wonderful. His relations as mentioned
in the Bible are overlooked almost entirely until our wants are discovered. When
these are made known and the soul begins in earnest to inquire after a remedy,
it needs not inquire in vain. "Say not in
thine heart, Who shall ascend up to heaven? that is, to bring down Christ from
above; or, Who shall descend into the
deep? that is, to bring Christ again from
the dead. But what saith it? The word
is nigh thee, even in thy mouth, and in
thy heart."

XVIII. *Christ as having all power or authority in heaven and earth*, needs also to be revealed to the soul, and received by faith, to dwell in and rule over it. The corresponding want must of necessity be first known to the mind before it can apprehend and appropriate Christ by faith in this or any other relation. The soul needs to see and feel its weakness, its need of protection, of being defended, and watched over, and controlled. It needs to see this, and also the power of its spiritual enemies, its besetments, its dangers and its certain ruin, unless the Almighty One interpose in its behalf. It needs thus truly and deeply to know itself, and then to inspire it with confidence, it needs a revelation of Christ as God, as the Almighty God, to the soul, as one who possesses absolute and infinite power, and as presented to the soul to be accepted as its strength and as all it needs of power.

Oh, how infinitely blind he is to the fullness and glory of Christ, who does not know himself and know Christ as both are revealed by the Holy Spirit. When we are led by the Holy Spirit to look down into the abyss of our own emptiness—to behold the horrible pit and miry clay of our own habits, and fleshly, and worldly, and infernal entanglements; when we see in the light of God that our emptiness and necessities are infinite; then, and not till then, are we prepared wholly to cast off self and to put on Christ. The glory and fullness of Christ are not discovered to the soul until it discovers its need of him. But when self in all its loathsomeness and helplessness, is fully revealed, until hope is utterly extinct as it respects every kind and degree of help in ourselves; and when Christ, the all in all, is revealed to the soul as its all-sufficient portion and salvation, then and not till then, does the soul know its salvation. This knowledge is the indispensable condition of appropriating faith, or of the act of receiving Christ, or that committal of all to him that takes Christ home to dwell in the heart by faith, and to preside over all its states and actions. Oh, such a knowledge and such a reception and putting on of Christ is blessed. Happy is he who knows it by his own experience.

It is indispensable to a steady and implicit faith that the soul should have a spiritual apprehension of what is implied in the saying of Christ that all power was delivered unto him. The ability of Christ to do all and even exceeding abundantly above all that we ask or think, is what the soul needs clearly to apprehend in a spiritual sense, that is, to apprehend it, not merely as a theory or a proposition, but to see the true spiritual import of this saying. This is also equally true of all that is said in the Bible about Christ, of all his offices and relations. It is one

3*

thing to theorize and speculate and opine about Christ, and an infinitely different thing to *know* him as he is revealed by the Holy Spirit. When Christ is fully revealed to the soul by the Comforter, it will never again doubt the attainability and reality of entire sanctification in this life.

XIX. Another necessity of the soul is to know Christ spiritually as the Prince of Peace. "Peace I leave with you; my peace I give unto you," said Christ. What is this peace? And who is Christ in the relation of the Prince of Peace? What is it to possess the peace of Christ— to have the *peace of God rule in your hearts?* Without the revelation of Christ to the soul by the Holy Spirit, it has no spiritual apprehension of the meaning of this language. Nor can it lay hold on and appropriate Christ as its peace, as the Prince of Peace. Whoever knows and has embraced Christ as his peace and as the Prince of Peace, knows what it is to have the peace of God *rule in his heart*. But none else at all understand the true spiritual import of this language, nor can it be so explained to them as that they will apprehend it unless it be explained by the Holy Spirit.

XX. The soul needs also to know Christ as the *Captain of Salvation*, as the skillful conductor, guide and captain of the soul in all its conflicts with its spiritual enemies, as one who is ever at hand to lead the soul on to victory and make it more than a conqueror in all its conflicts with the world, the flesh, and Satan. How indispensable to a living and efficient faith it is, and must be for the soul to clearly apprehend by the Holy Spirit, this relation of Captain of Salvation and Captain of the Lord's Host. Without confidence in the Leader and Captain, how shall the soul put itself under his guidance and protection in the hour of conflict? It can not.

The fact is that when the soul is ignorant of Christ as a Captain or Leader, it will surely fall in battle. If the church as a body but knew the Captain of the Lord's Host; if he were but truly and spiritually known to them in that relation, no more confusion would be seen in the ranks of God's elect. All would be order and strength and conquest. They would soon go up and take possession of the whole territory that has been promised to Christ. The heathen would soon be given to him for an inheritance and the uttermost part of the world for a possession. Joshua knew Christ as the Captain of the Lord's Host. Consequently he had more courage, and efficiency, and prowess, than all Israel besides. Even so it is now. When a soul can be found who thoroughly knows and has embraced and appropriated Christ, he is a host of himself. That is, he has appropriated the attributes of Christ to himself; and his influence is felt in heaven, and earth, and hell.

XXI. Another affecting and important relation in which the soul needs to know Christ, is that of our Passover.

It needs to understand that the only reason why it has not been or will not assuredly be slain for sin is that Christ has sprinkled, as our Paschal Lamb, the lintel and door-posts of our souls with his own blood, and that therefore the destroying angel passes us by. There is a most deep and sin-subduing, or rather temptation-subduing spirituality in this relation of Christ to the soul when revealed by the Holy Spirit. We must apprehend our sins as slaying the Lamb, and apply his blood to our souls by faith—his blood as being our protection and our only trust. We need to know the security there is in this being sprinkled with his blood, and the certain and speedy destruction of all who have not taken refuge under it. We need to know also that it will not do for a moment to venture out into the streets and from under its protection, lest we be slain there.

XXII. To know Christ as our Wisdom in the true spiritual sense is doubtless indispensable to our entire, in the sense of continued, sanctification. He is our Wisdom in the sense of being the whole of our religion. That is, when separated from him we have no spiritual life whatever. He is at the bottom of, or the inducing cause of all our obedience. This we need clearly to apprehend. Until the soul clearly understands this, it has learned nothing to the purpose of its helplessness and of Christ's spiritual relations to it.

XXIII. Very nearly allied to this is Christ's relation to the soul as its Sanctification. I have been amazed at the ignorance of the church and of the ministry respecting *Christ as its Sanctification.* He is not its *Sanctifier* in the sense that he does something to the soul that enables it to stand and persevere in holiness in its own strength. He does not change the structure of the soul, but he watches over and works in it to will and to do *continually*, and thus becomes its *Sanctification*. His influence is not exerted once for all, but constantly. When he is apprehended and embraced as the soul's sanctification, he rules in and reigns over the soul in so high a sense that he, as it were, develops his own holiness in us. He, as it were swallows us up, so enfolds (if I may so say,) our wills and our souls in his, that we are willingly led captive by him. We will and do as he wills within us. He charms the will into a universal bending to his will. He so establishes his throne in, and his authority over us that he subdues us to himself. He becomes our sanctification only in so far forth as we are revealed to ourselves, and he revealed to us, and as we receive him and put him on. What! has it come to this, that the church doubt and reject the doctrine of entire sanctification in this life?

Then, it must be that they have lost sight of Christ as their sanctification. Is not Christ perfect in all his relations? Is there not a completeness and fullness in him? When embraced by us are we not complete in him? The secret of all this doubting about and opposition to the doctrine of entire sanctification is to be found in the fact that Christ is not apprehended and embraced as *our sanctification*. The Holy Spirit sanctifies only by revealing Christ to us as our sanctification. He does not speak of himself, but takes of the things of Christ and shows them to us.

Two among the most prominent ministers of the Presbyterian church have said to me within a few years that they had never heard of Christ as the sanctification of the soul. O, how many of the ministry of the present day overlook the true spiritual gospel of Christ!

XXIV. Another of Christ's spiritual relations is that of the Redemption of the soul; not merely as the *Redeemer* conside.ed in his governmental relation, but as a present *Redemption*. To apprehend and receive Christ in this relation, the soul needs to apprehend itself as sold under sin; as being the voluntary but real slave of lust and appetite, except as Christ continually delivers us from its power by strengthening and confirming our wills in resisting and overcoming the flesh.

XXV. Christ our Prophet is another important spiritual relation in which we need to apprehend Christ by the Holy Spirit as a condition of entire sanctification. He must be received as the great teacher of our souls, so that every word of his will be received as God speaking to us. This will render the Bible precious, and all the words of life efficient to the sanctification of our souls.

XXVI. As our High Priest we need also to know Christ. I say we need to know him in this relation as really ever living and sustaining this relation to us,

offering up, as it were, by a continual offering, his own blood and himself, as a
propitiation for our sins; as being entered within the veil and as ever living to
make intercession for us. Much precious
instruction is to be gathered from this relation of Christ. We need, perishingly
need, to know Christ in this relation, as
a condition of a right dependence upon
him. I all the while feel embarassed with
the consideration that I am not able in
this course of instruction to give a fuller
account of Christ in these relations. We
need a distinct revelation of him in each
of these relations in order to a thorough
understanding and clear apprehension of
that which is implied in each and all of
the relations of Christ.

When we sin, it is because of our ignorance of Christ. That is, whenever
temptation overcomes us, it is because
we do not know and avail ourselves of
that relation of Christ that would meet
at the time our necessities. One great

thing that needs to be done is to correct the developments of our sensibility. The appetites and passions are enormously developed in their relations to earthly objects. In relation to things of time and sense our propensities are greatly developed and are alive; but in relation to spiritual truths and objects and eternal realities, we are naturally as dead as stones. When first converted, if we knew enough of ourselves and of Christ to thoroughly develop and correct the action of the sensibility and confirm our wills in a state of entire consecration, we should not fall. In proportion as the law-work preceding conversion has been thorough and the revelation of Christ at or immediately subsequent to conversion full and clear, just in that proportion do we witness stability in converts. In most, if not in all instances, however, the convert is too ignorant of himself, and, of course, knows too little about Christ, to be established in permanent obedience.

He needs renewed conviction of sin, to be revealed to himself and to have Christ revealed to him, and be formed in him the hope of glory, before he will be steadfast, always abounding in the work of the Lord.

Before I close this chapter, 1 must remark and shall have occasion to repeat the remark, that from what has been said, it must not be inferred that the knowledge of Christ in all these relations is a condition of our coming into our state of entire consecration to God or of present sanctification. The thing insisted on is that the soul will abide in this state in the hour of temptation only so far forth as it betakes itself to Christ in such circumstances of trial, and apprehends and appropriates Him by faith, from time to time in those relations that meet the present and pressing necessities of the soul. The temptation is the occasion of revealing the necessity, and the Holy Spirit is always ready to reveal Christ, in the particular relation suited to the newly developed necessity. The perception and appropriation of 'Him in this relation, under these circumstances of trial, is the *sine qua non* of our remaining in the state of entire consecration.

CHAPTER III.

XXVII. We need also to know ourselves as starving souls, and Christ as the
" Bread of Life," as "the Bread that came
down from Heaven." We need to know
spiritually and experimentally what it is
to " eat of his flesh and to drink of his
blood," to *receive* Him as the bread of life,
to *appropriate* Him to the nourishment of
our souls as really as we appropriate bread,
by digestion to the nourishment of our
bodies. This I know is mysticism to the
carnal professor. But to the truly spiritually minded, "this is the bread of God
that came down from heaven, of which if
a man eat he shall never die." To hear

Christ talk of eating his flesh and of drinking his blood was a great stumbling-block to the carnal Jews, as it is now to carnal professors. Nevertheless this is a glorious truth that Christ is the constant sustenance of the spiritual life as truly and as lite rally as food is the sustenance of the body. But the soul will never eat this bread until it has ceased to attempt to fill itself with the husks of its own doings, or with any provision this world can furnish. Do you know, Christian, what it is to eat of this bread? If so, then you will never die.

XXVIII. Christ also needs to be revealed to the soul as the fountain of the water of life. "If any man thirst," says He, "let him come unto me and drink." " I am the Alpha and Omega, and to him that is athirst will I give to drink of the fountain of the water of life freely." The soul needs to have such discoveries made to it, as to beget a thirst after God, that cannot be allayed except by a copious draft at the fountain of the water of life.

It is indispensable to the establishing of
the soul in perfect love, that its hunger-
ing after the bread and its thirsting for
the water of life should be duly enkindled,
and that the spirit should pant and struggle after God, and " cry out for the living
God," that it should be able to say with
truth : " My soul panteth after God as the
hart panteth after the water brooks;" "My
heart and my flesh cry out for the living
God;" " My soul breaketh for the longing that it hath after thee at all times."
When this state of mind is induced by the
Holy Spirit so that the longing of the soul
after perpetual holiness is irrepressible, it
is prepared for a revelation of Christ in all
those offices and relations that are necessary to secure its establishment in love.
Especially is it then prepared to apprehend, appreciate and appropriate Christ
as the bread and water of life, to understand what it is to eat the flesh and drink
the blood of the Son of God.   It is then in
a state to understand what Christ meant

when He said, "Blessed are they that do
hunger and thirst after righteousness, for
they shall be filled." They not only understand what it is to hunger and thirst,
but also what it is to be filled; to have
the hunger and thirst allayed, and the
largest desire fully satisfied. The soul
then realizes, in its own experience, the
truthfulness of the apostle's saying, that
Christ "is able to do exceedingly abundantly above all that we ask or think."
Many stop short even of any thing like in-
tense hunger and thirst; others hunger and
thirst, but have not the idea of the perfect
fullness and adaptedness of Christ to meet
and satisfy the longing of their souls.
They, therefore, do not plead and look for
the soul-satisfying revelation of Christ.
They expect no such divine fullness and
satisfaction of soul. They are ignorant of
the fullness and perfection of the pro-
visions of the "glorious gospel of the blessed God," and consequently they are not
encouraged to hope, from the fact that
4

they hunger and thirst after righteousness that they shall be filled ; but they remain unfed, unfilled, unsatisfied, and after a season, through unbelief, fall into indifference and remain in bondage to lust.

XXIX. *The soul also needs to know Christ as the true God, and the eternal life.* " No man can say that Jesus is the Lord save by the Holy Spirit." The proper divinity of Christ is never and never can be held otherwise than as a mere opinion, a tenet, a speculation, an article of a creed, until He is revealed to the inner man by the Holy Spirit. But nothing short of an apprehension of Christ as the supreme and living God to the soul can inspire that confidence in Him that is essential to its established sanctification. The soul can have no apprehension of what was intended by his being the "Eternal Life," until it spiritually knows Him as the true God. When He is spiritually revealed as the true and living God, the way is prepared for the spiritual apprehension of Him as the eternal life. "As the living Father hath life in Himself, so hath he given to the Son to have life in Himself." "In Him was life and the life was the light of men." "I give unto them eternal life." "I am the way, the truth, and the life." "I am the resurrection and the life." These and similar passages the soul needs spiritually to apprehend, to have a spiritual and personal revelation of them within. Most professors seem to me to have no right idea of the condition upon which the Bible can be made of spiritual use to them. They seem not to understand that in its letter it is only a history of things formerly revealed to men; that it is a fact, a revelation to no man except upon the condition of its being personally revealed, or revealed to us in particular by the Holy Spirit. The mere fact that we have in the gospel the history of the birth, the life, the death of Christ, is no such revelation of Christ to any man as meets his necessities and as will insure or render his salvation possible. Christ and his doctrine, his life, and death, and resurrection, need to be revealed personally by the Holy Spirit, to each and every soul of man to effect his salvation. So it is with every spiritual truth; without an inward revelation of it to the soul, it is only a savor of death unto death. It is in vain to hold to the proper divinity of Christ as a speculation, a doctrine, a theory, an opinion, without the revelation of his divine nature and character to the soul by the Holy Spirit. But let the soul know Him and walk with Him as the true God, and then it will no longer question whether, as our sanctification, He is all-sufficient and complete. Let no one object to this that if this is true, men are under no obligation to believe in Christ and to obey the gospel without or until they are enlightened by the Holy Spirit. To such an objection, should it be made, I would answer,

CHRIST THE TRUE LIGHT.

1. Men are under an obligation to believe every truth so far as they can understand or apprehend it, but no farther. So far as they can apprehend the spiritual truths of the gospel without the Holy Spirit, so far, without his aid, they are bound to believe it. But Christ has Himself taught us that no man can come to Him except the Father draw him. That this drawing means teaching is evident from what Christ proceeds to say: "For it is written," said He, "they shall all be taught of God. Every one therefore that hath heard and hath learned of the Father cometh to me." That this learning of the Father is something different from the mere oral or written instructions of Christ and the apostles, is evident from the fact that Christ assured those to whom He preached with all the plainness with which He was able, that they still could not come to Him except drawn, that is taught of the Father. As the Father teaches by the Holy Spirit, Christ's plain

teaching in the passage under consideration is, that no man can come to Him except he be specially enlightened by the
Holy Spirit. Paul unequivocally teaches
the same thing. " No man," says he,
" can say that Jesus is the Lord but by
the Holy Spirit." Notwithstanding all
teaching of the apostles, no man by merely
listening to their instruction could so apprehend the true divinity of Christ as to
honestly and with spiritual understanding
say that Jesus is the Lord. But what
spiritual or true Christian does not know
the radical difference between being
taught of man and of God, between the
opinions that we form from reading, hearing and study, and the clear apprehensions of truth that are communicated by
the direct and inward illuminations of the
Holy Spirit.

2. I answer that men under the gospel
are entirely without excuse for not enjoying all the light they need from the Holy
Spirit, since He is in the world, has been

sent for the very purpose of giving to all,
all the knowledge of themselves and of
Christ which they need. His aid is freely
proffered to all, and Christ has assured us
that the Father is more willing to give
the Holy Spirit to them that ask Him
than parents are to give good gifts to
their children. All men under the gospel
know this and all men have light enough
to ask in faith for the Holy Spirit, and of
course all men may know of themselves
and of Christ all that they need to know.
They are therefore able to know and to
embrace Christ as fully and as fast as it
is their duty to embrace him. They are
able to know Christ in his governmental
and spiritual relations just as fast as they
come into circumstances to need to know
Him in these various relations. The
Holy Spirit, if He is not quenched and re-
sisted, will surely reveal Christ in all his
relations and fullness in due time, so that
in every temptation a way of escape will
be open, so that we shall be able to bear

¡t. This is expressly promised, 1 Cor. 10 : 13. " There hath no temptation taken you but such as are common to man; but God is, faithful, who will not suffer you to be tempted above that ye are able, but will with the temptation also make a way to escape, that ye may be able to bear it." Men are able to know what God offers to teach them upon a condition within the compass of their ability. The Holy Spirit offers, upon condition of faith in the express promise of God to lead every man into all truth. Every man is therefore under obligation to know and do the whole truth so far and so fast as it is possible for him to do so with the light of the Holy Spirit.

XXX. But be it remembered that it is not enough for us to *apprehend* Christ as the true God and the eternal life, but we need also to lay hold upon Him as *our life*. It can not be too distinctly understood that a particular and personal appropriation of Christ in such relations is indispensable to our being rooted and grounded, established and perfected in love. When our utter deficiency and emptiness in any one respect or direction is deeply revealed to us by the Holy Spirit with the corresponding remedy and perfect fullness in Christ, it then remains for the soul in this respect and direction to cast off self and put on Christ. When this is done, when self in that respect and direction is dead, and Christ is risen and lives and reigns in the heart in that relation, all is strong, and whole, and complete in that department of our life and experience. For example, suppose we find ourselves constitutionally, or by reason of our relations and circumstances, exposed to certain besetments and temptations that overcome us. Our weakness in this respect we observe in our experience. But upon observing our exposedness and experiencing something of our weakness, we begin with piling resolution upon resolution. We bind ourselves with

4*

oaths, and promises, and covenants, but all in vain. When we purpose to stand, we invariably, in the presence of the temptation, fall. This process of resolving and falling brings the soul into great discouragement and perplexity, until at last the Holy Spirit reveals to us fully that we are attempting to stand and to build upon nothing. The utter emptiness and worse than uselessness of our resolutions and self-originated efforts, is so clearly seen by us as to annihilate forever self-dependence in this respect. Now the soul is prepared for the revelation of Christ to meet this particular want. Christ is revealed and apprehended as the soul's substitute, surety, life and salvation in respect to the particular besetment and weakness of which it has had so full and so humiliating a revelation. Now if the soul utterly and forever cast off and renounce self, and put on the Lord Jesus Christ as He is seen to be needed to meet his necessity, then all is complete in Him.

Thus far Christ is reigning within us. Thus far we know what is the power of his resurrection, and are made comformable to his death.

But I said that we need to know and to lay hold upon Christ as *our life*. Too much stress cannot be laid upon our personal responsibility to Christ, our individual relation to Him, our personal interest in Him, and obligation to Him. To sanctify *our own* souls, we need to make every department of religion a personal matter between us and God, to regard every precept of the Bible, and every promise, saying, exhortation, threatening, and in short, we need to regard the whole Bible as given to *us*, and earnestly seek the personal revelation of every truth it contains to our own souls. No one can too fully understand or too deeply feel the necessity of taking home the Bible with all it contains as a message sent from heaven to *him*, nor can he too earnestly desire or seek the promised Spirit to teach him the true spiritual import of all its contents. O, he must have the Bible become a personal revelation of God to his own soul. It must become his own book. He must know Christ for himself. He must know Him in his different relations. He must know Him in his blessed and infinite fullness, or he can not abide in Him, and unless he abide in Christ, he can bring forth none of the fruits of holiness. "Except a man abide in me he is cast forth as a branch and is withered."

Apprehending and embracing Christ as our life, implies the apprehension of the fact that we of ourselves are dead in trespasses and in sins, that we have no life in ourselves, that death has reigned and will eternally reign in and over us unless Christ become our life. Until man knows himself to be dead, and that he is wholly destitute of spiritual life in himself, he will never know Christ as his life. It is not enough to hold the *opinion* that all men are by nature dead in trespasses and sins.

It is not enough to hold the opinion that *we* are in common with all men, in this condition in and of ourselves. We must *see* it. We must know what such language means. It must be made a matter of personal revelation to us. We must be made fully to apprehend our own death and Christ as our life, and we must fully recognize *our* death and *Him* as *our* life by personally renouncing self in this respect and laying hold on Him as *our own spiritual and eternal life.* Many persons, and strange to say, some eminent ministers, are so blinded as to suppose that a soul entirely sanctified does not any longer need Christ, assuming that such a soul has spiritual life in and of himself; that there is in him some foundation or efficient occasion of continued holiness, as if the Holy Spirit had changed his nature or infused physical holiness or a holy principle into him. O, when will such men cease to darken counsel by words without knowledge upon the infinitely

important subject of sanctification! When
will such men—when will the church,
understand that Christ is our sanctification; that we have no life, no holiness, no
sanctification, except as we abide in Christ
and He in us; that separate from Christ,
there never is any moral excellence in any
man; that Christ does not change the
constitution of man in sanctification, but
that He only, by our own consent, gains
and keeps the heart; that He enthrones
Himself, with our consent, in the heart, and
through the heart He extends his influence
and his life to all our spiritual being; that
He lives in us as really and truly as we
live in our own bodies; that He as really
reigns in our will and consequently in our
emotions, by our own free consent, as our
wills reign in our bodies? Can not our
brethren understand that this is sanctification, and that nothing else is? that
there is no degree of sanctification that is
not to be thus ascribed to Christ? and
that entire sanctification is nothing else

than the reign of Jesus in the soul? nothing more nor less than Christ the resurrection and the life, raising the soul from spiritual death, and reigning in it through righteousness unto eternal life? I must know and embrace Christ as my life; I must abide in him as a branch abides in the vine; I must not only hold this opinion as an opinion; I must know and act on it in practice. O, when the ministry of reconciliation all know and embrace a whole Christ for themselves; when they preach Jesus in all his fullness and present vital power to the church; when they testify what they have seen and their hands have handled of the word of life— then and not till then will there be a general resurrection of the dry bones of the house of Israel. Amen. Lord, hasten the day.

XXXI. We need especially to know Christ as the "All in all." Col. 3: 11; " Where there is neither Greek nor Jew, circumcision nor uncircumcision, barbarian, Scythian, bond nor free, but Christ is all and in all." Before the soul will cease to be overcome by temptation, it must renounce self-dependence in all things. It must be as it were self-annihilated. It must cease to *think* of self as having in it any ground of dependence in the hour of trial. It must wholly and in all things renounce self and put on Christ. It must know self as *nothing* in the matter of spiritual life, and Christ as all. The Psalmist could say, " all our springs are in thee." He is the fountain of life. Whatever of life is in us flows directly from Him as the sap flows from the vine to the branch, or a rivulet flows from its fountain. The spiritual life that is in us is really Christ's life flowing through us. Our activity, though properly our own, is nevertheless stimulated and directed by his presence and agency within us. So that we can and must say with Paul, " yet not I, but Christ liveth in me."—Gal. 2: 20. It is a good thing for a self-conceited sinner to

suffer even in his own view, self-annihila-
tion as it respects the origination of any
spiritual obedience to God, or any spiritual good whatever. But this must be before he will learn on all occasions and in
all things to stand in Christ, to abide in
Him as his "ALL." O, the infinite folly
and madness of the carnal mind! It
would seem that it will always make trial
of its own strength before it will depend
on Christ. It will look first for resources
and help within itself before it will renounce self and make Christ its "al lin
all." It will betake itself to its own wisdom, righteousness, sanctification, and redemption. In short, there is not an office
or relation of Christ that will be recognized and embraced, until the soul has first
come into circumstances to have its wants
in relation to that office of Christ developed by some trial, often by some fall under temptation. It will not be embraced,
until in addition to this Christ is clearly and
prevailingly revealed by the Holy Spirit

insomuch that self is put down and Christ is exalted in the heart. Sin has so becrazed and befooled mankind that when Christ tells them, "without me ye can do nothing; and if any man abide not in me, he is cast forth as a branch and is withered," they neither apprehend what or how much He means, and how much is really implied in these and similar sayings, until one trial after another fully develops the appalling fact that they are nothing so far as spiritual good is concerned, and that Christ is *"all and in all."*

XXXII. Another relation in which the soul must know Christ, before it will steadily abide in Him, is that of " the Resurrection and the Life." Through and by Christ the soul is raised from spiritual death. Christ as the resurrection and the life is raised in the soul. He arises or revives the divine image out of the spiritual death that reigns within us. He is begotten by the Holy Spirit and born within us. He arises through the death that is within us and develops his own life within our own being. Will any one say, " this is a hard saying, who can hear it?" Until we know by our own experience the power of this resurrection within us, we shall never understand " the fellowship of his sufferings, and be made conformable to his death." He raises our will from its fallen state of death in trespasses and sins, or from its state of committal and voluntary enslavement to lust and self, to a state of conformity to the will of God. Through the intelligence, He pours a stream of quickening truth upon the soul. He thus quickens the will into obedience. By making fresh discoveries to the soul, He strengthens and confirms the will in obedience. By thus raising, and sustaining, and quickening the will, He rectifies the sensibility, and quickens and raises the whole man from the dead, or rather builds up a new and spiritual man upon the death and ruins of the old and carnal man. He

raises the same powers and faculties that
were dead in trespasses and sins to a
spiritual life. He overcomes their death
and inspires them with life. He lives in
saints, and works in them to will and to
do, and they live in Him according to the
saying of Christ, in his address to his
Father, Jno. 17 : 21. "As thou, Father,
art in me, and I in thee, that they also
may be one in us;" and again, 23: "I in
them and thou in me, that they may be
made perfect in one." He does not raise
the soul to spiritual life in any such sense
that it has life separate from Him for one
moment. The spiritual resurrection is
a continual one. Christ is the resurrection in the sense that He is at the foundation of all our obedience at every moment.
He, as it were, raises the soul or the will
from the slavery of lust to a conformity
to the will of God in every instance
and at every moment of its consecration
to the will of God. But this He does
only upon condition of our apprehending

and embracing him in this relation. In reading the Bible, I have often been struck with the fact that the inspired writers were far ahead of the great mass of professed believers. They write of the relations in which Christ had been spiritually revealed to them. All the names and titles, and official relations of Christ must have had great significancy with them. They spoke not from theory or from what man had taught them, but from experience, from what the Holy Spirit taught them. As the risen Christ is risen and lives, and is developed in one relation after another, in the experience of believers, how striking the writings of inspiration appear! As the necessities of our being are developed in experience, and as Christ is revealed as in all new circumstances and relations, just that and all that we need, who has not marveled to find in the Bible, way-marks and guide-boards and mile-stones, and all the evidences that we could ask or desire that inspired men have gone this way and have had substantially the same experience that we have. We are often also struck with the fact that they are so far ahead of us. At every stage in our progress we seem to have, as it were, a new and improved edition of the Bible. We discover worlds of truth before unnoticed by us—come to know Christ in precious relations in which we had known nothing of Him before. And ever, as our real wants are discovered, Christ is seen to be all that we need, just the thing that exactly and fully meets the necessities of our souls. This is indeed " the glorious gospel of the blessed God."

XXXIII. Another precious and most influential relation of Christ in the affair of our sanctification, is that of the Bridegroom or Husband of the soul. The individual soul needs to be espoused to Christ, to enter this relation personally by its own consent. Mere earthly and outward marriages are nothing but sin, unless the hearts are married. True marriage is of the heart, and the outward ceremony is only a public manifestation or profession of the union or marriage of souls or hearts.

All marriage may be regarded as typical of that union into which the soul enters with Christ. This relation of Christ with the soul is frequently recognized both in the Old and New Testament. It is treated of by Paul as a great mystery. The seventh and eighth chapters of Romans present a striking illustration of the results of the soul's remaining under the law on the one hand, and of its being married to Christ on the other. The seventh chapter begins thus, "Know ye not brethren, (for I speak to them that know the law,) how that the law hath dominion over a man as long as he liveth? For the woman who hath a husband is bound by the law to her husband so long as he liveth; but if her husband be dead she is loosed from the law of her husband. So then, if while her husband liveth, she be married to another man, she shall be called an adulteress; but if her husband be dead she is free from that law so that she is no adulteress though she be married to another man. Therefore, my brethren, ye also are become dead to the law by the body of Christ, that ye should be married to another, even to Christ who was raised from the dead, that we should bring forth fruit unto God." The apostle then proceeds to show the results of these two marriages or relations of the soul. When married to the law he says of it, "For when we were in the flesh the motions of sins, which were by the law, did work in our members to bring forth fruit unto death." But when married to Christ he proceeds to say, "We are delivered from the law, that being dead wherein we were held; that we should serve in newness of spirit and not in the oldness of the letter." The remaining part of this (7th) chapter is occupied with an account of the soul's bondage while married to the law ; of its efforts to please its husband ; with its continual failures ; its deep convictions; its selfish efforts; its consciousness of failures, and its consequent self-condemnation and despondency.. It is perfectly obvious, when the allegory with which the apostle commences this chapter is considered, that he is portraying a legal experience for the purpose of contrasting it with the experience of one who has attained to the true liberty of perfect love.

The eighth chapter represents the results of the marriage of the soul to Christ. It is delivered from its bondage to the law and from the power of the law of sin in the members. It brings forth fruit unto God. Christ has succeeded in gaining the affections of the soul. What the law could not do, Christ has done, and the righteousness of the law is now fulfilled in the soul. The representation is as follows: The soul is married to the law and

5

acknowledges its obligation to obey its husband. The husband requires perfect love to God and man. The love is wanting; the soul is selfish. This displeases the husband, and he denounces death against her if she does not love. She recognizes the reasonableness of both the requisition and the threatening, and resolves upon full obedience. But being selfish, the command and threatening but increase the difficulty. All her efforts at obedience are for selfish reasons. The husband is justly firm and imperative in his demands. The wife trembles, and promises, and resolves upon obedience. But all in vain. Her obedience is only feigned, outward and not love. She becomes disheartened and gives up in despair. As sentence is about to be executed Christ appears. He witnesses the dilemma. He reveres, and honors, and loves the husband. He entirely approves his requisition and the course he has taken. He condemns in most unqualified terms the wife. Still He pities and loves her with deep benevolence. He will consent to nothing that shall have the appearance of disapproving the claims or the course of her husband. His rectitude must be openly acknowledged. Her husband must not be dishonored. But on the contrary he must be "magnified and made honorable." Still Christ so much pities the wife, as to be willing to die as her substitute. This He does, and the wife is regarded as dying in and. by Him her substitute. Now since a death of either of the parties is a dissolution of the marriage covenant, and since the wife in the person of her substitute has died under and to the law, her husband, she is now at liberty to marry again. Christ rises from the dead. This striking and overpowering manifestation of disinterested benevolence on the part of Christ in dying for her, subdues her selfishness and wins her whole heart. He proposes marriage and she consents with her whole soul. Now she finds the law of selfishness or of self-gratification broken, and the righteousness of the law of love fulfilled in her heart. The last husband requires just what the first required, but having won her whole heart, she no longer needs to resolve to love, for love is as natural and spontaneous as her breath. Before, the 7th of Romans was the language of her *complaint*. Now the eighth is the language of her *triumph*. Before, she found herself unable to meet the demands of her husband, and equally unable to satisfy her own conscience. Now she finds it easy to obey her husband and that his commandments are not grievous, although they are identical with those of the first husband. Now this allegory of the apostle is not a mere rhetorical flourish. It represents a reality, and one of the most important and glorious realities in existence, namely, the real and spiritual union of the soul to Christ, and the blessed results of this union, the bringing forth of fruit unto

God. This union is, as the apostle says, a great mystery; nevertheless it is a glorious reality. "He that is joined unto the Lord is one spirit."—1 Cor. 6: 17.

Now until the soul knows what it is to be married to the law and is able to adopt the language of the seventh of Romans, it is not prepared to see, and appreciate, and be properly affected by the death and love of Christ. Great multitudes rest in this first marriage, and do not consent to die and rise again in Christ. They are not married to Christ and do not know that there is such a thing, and expect to live and die in this bondage, crying out, "O wretched man that I am!" They need to die and rise again in Christ to a new life founded in and growing out of a new relation to Christ. Christ becomes the living head or husband of the soul, its surety, its life. He gains and retains the deepest affection of the soul, thus writing his law in the heart and engraving it in the inward parts.

But not only must the soul know what it is to be married to the law with its consequent thraldom and death, but it must also for itself enter into the marriage relation with a risen, living Christ. This must not be theory, an opinion, a tenet ; nor must it be an imagination, a mysticism, a notion, a dream.   It must be a living, personal, real entering into a personal and living union with Christ, a most entire and universal giving of self to Him and receiving of Him in the relation of spiritual husband and head.   The Spirit of Christ and our spirit must embrace each other and enter into an everlasting covenant with each other.   There must be a mutual giving of self and receiving of each other, a blending of spirits in such a sense as is intended by Paul in the passage already quoted: " He that is joined to the Lord is one spirit."

My brother, my sister, do you understand this? Do you know what both these marriages are, with their diverse results ? If you do not, make no longer pretense to being sanctified, for you are still in the gall of bitterness and in the bond of iniquity. " Escape for thy life."

CHAPTER IV.

XXXIV. Another interesting and highly important relation which Christ sustains to his people, is that of *Shepherd*. This relation presupposes the helpless and defenceless condition of Christians in this life, and the indispensable necessity of guardianship and protection. Christ was revealed to the Psalmist in this relation, and when on earth, He revealed Himself to his disciples in this relation. It is not enough, however, that he should be revealed merely in the letter or in words as sustaining this relation. The real spiritual import of this relation and what is implied in it, needs to be revealed by the Holy Spirit, to give to it efficiency, and beget that universal trust in the presence, care, and protection of Christ, that is often essential to preventing a fall in the hour of temptation. Christ meant all that He said when He professed to be the Good Shepherd, that cared for the sheep, that would not flee, but that would lay down his life for them. In this relation, as in all others, there is infinite fullness and perfection. If the sheep do thoroughly know and confide in the Shepherd, they will follow Him, will flee to Him for protection in every hour of danger, will at all times depend on Him for all things. Now all this is received and possessed in theory by all professors of religion. And yet how few comparatively seem to have had Christ so revealed to them as to have secured the actual embracing of Him in this relation and a continual dependence on Him for all that is implied in it. Now either this is a vain boast of Christ, or else He may be and ought to be depended upon, and the soul has a right to throw itself upon

5*

Him for all that is implied in the relation of *Good Shepherd*.   But this relation with all the other relations of Christ, implies a corresponding necessity in us. This necessity we must see and feel, or this relation of Christ will have no impressive significancy. We need, then, in this case as in all others, the revelation of the Holy Spirit to make us thoroughly to apprehend our dependence, and to reveal Christ in the Spirit and fullness of this relation, and to urge our acceptance home upon us until our souls have thoroughly closed with Him. Some fall into the mistake of supposing that when their necessities and the fullness of Christ have been revealed to the mind by the Spirit, the work is done. But unless they actually receive Him and commit themselves to Him in this relation, they will soon find to their shame that nothing has been done to purpose so far as their standing in the hour of temptation is concerned. He may be clearly revealed in any of his relations, the soul may see both its necessities and his fullness and yet forget or neglect to actively and personally receive Him in these relations. It should never be forgotten that this is in every case indispensable. The revelation is designed to secure our acceptance of Him; if it does not do this, it has only greatly aggravated our guilt without at all securing to us the benefits of these relations. It is amazing to see how common it is and has been for ministers to overlook this truth, and of course neither to practice it themselves, nor urge it upon their hearers. Hence Christ is not known to multitudes, and is not in many cases received even when He is revealed by the Holy Spirit. If I am not greatly mistaken, thorough inquiry would show that error upon this subject exists to a most appalling extent. The personal and individual acceptance of Christ in all his offices and relations as the *sine qua non*

of entire sanctification, seems to me to
be seldom either understood or insisted
on by ministers of the present day, and
of course little thought of by the church.
The idea of accepting for ourselves a
whole Savior, of appropriating to our
own individual selves all the offices and
relations of Jesus, seems to be a rare
idea in this age of the church. But for
what purpose does He sustain these relations? Is the bare apprehension of those
truths and of Christ in the relations
enough, without our own activity being
duly excited by the apprehension, to lay
hold and avail ourselves of his fullness?
What folly and madness for the church to
expect to be saved by a rejected Savior!
To what purpose is it for the Spirit to
make Him known to us, unless we as individuals embrace Him and make Him our
own? Let the soul but truly and fully
apprehend and embrace Christ in this relation of Shepherd, and it shall never per-
ish, neither shall any pluck it out of his

hand. The knowing of Christ in this relation, secures the soul against following strangers. But thus knowing Him is indispensable to securing this result. If we know him as Shepherd, we shall follow Him, but not else. Let this be well considered.

XXXV. Christ is also the *Door* by and through which the soul enters the fold and finds security and protection among the sheep. This needs also to be spiritually apprehended, and the door needs to be spiritually and personally answered to secure the guardianship of the Good Shepherd. Those who do not spiritually and truly apprehend Christ as the door, and enter by and through Him, and yet hope for salvation, are surely attempting to climb up some other way, and are therefore thieves and robbers. This is a familiar and well known truth, in the mouth not only of every minister and Christian, but of every Sabbath School child. Yet how few really apprehend and

embrace its spiritual import. That there
is no other means or way of access to the
fold of God, is admitted by all the orthodox; but who really perceives and knows
through the personal revelation of the
Holy Spirit, what and all Christ meant in
the very significant words, "Verily, verily,
I say unto you, I am the door of the
sheep;" " I am the door; by me if any
man enter in, he shall be saved, and shall
go in and out and find pasture?" He who
truly discovers this door, and gains access
by it, will surely realize in his own experience the faithfulness of the Good Shepherd, and will go in and out and find pasture. That is, he will surely be fed, be
led into green pastures and beside the still
waters.

But it is well to inquire, What is implied
in this relation of Christ?

1. It implies that we are shut out from
the protection and favor of God except
as we approach Him through and by
Christ.

2. It implies that we need to know and clearly to apprehend and appreciate this.

3. That we need to discover the door and what is implied both in the door and in entering it.

4. That entering it implies the utter renunciation of self and of self-righteousness and self-protection, and support, and a putting ourselves entirely under the control and protection of the Shepherd.

5. That we need the revelation of the Holy Spirit to make us clearly apprehend the true spiritual import of this relation and what is implied in it.

6. That when Christ is revealed in this relation, we need to embrace Him and for ourselves to enter by and through Him into the enclosure that every where surrounds the children of God.

It is an inward and not a mere outward revelation that we need. It is an inward, a heart-entering, and not a mere notion, idea, theory, dream of the imagi-

nation. It is really an intelligent act of
the mind; as much and as real an entering into the fold or favor of God, by and
through Christ as we ever entered the
house of God on the Sabbath day by the
door. When the soul enters by the door,
it finds an infinitely different reception
and treatment from that of those who
climb up into the church upon a ladder of
mere opinion, a scaling ladder of mere
orthodoxy. This last class are not fed.
They find no protection from the Good
Shepherd. They do not know the Shepherd and follow Him, because they have
climbed up another way. They have not
confidence in Him, can not approach Him
with boldness and claim his guardianship
and protection. Their knowledge of
Christ is but an opinion, a theory, a heart-
less and fruitless speculation. O, how
many give the saddest proof that they
have never entered by the door, and consequently have no realization in their own
life and experience of the blessed and

efficient protection and support of the Good Shepherd. Here I must not forget again to insist upon the necessity of a personal revelation of our relations to God as being excluded from all access to Him and his favor save through Christ the door; and also the necessity of the personal revelation to us by the Holy Spirit of Christ as the door, and of what is implied in this; and lastly and emphatically upon the indispensable necessity of a personal, responsible, active and full entering in at this door and gaining access for ourselves to the inclosure of the love and favor of God. Let this never for one moment be forgotten or overlooked. I must enter for and by myself. I must *truly* enter. I must be *conscious that I enter.* I must be sure that I do not misapprehend what is implied in entering; and at my peril I must not forget or neglect to enter.

And here it is important to inquire, have you had this personal and spiritual

revelation? Have you clearly seen yourself without the fold, exposed to all the
unrelenting cruelty of your spiritual enemies and shut out forever by your sin
from the favor and protection of God?
When this has been revealed, have you
been made clearly to apprehend Christ
as the door? Have you understood what
is implied in his sustaining this relation?
And last, but not least, have you entered
this door by faith? Have you seen the
door open, and have you entered for
yourself, and have you daily this evidence
that you follow the Shepherd, and find
all you need.

XXXVI. Christ is also the Way of
Salvation.

Observe: He is not a mere teacher of
the way, as some vainly imagine and
teach. Christ is truly " the way" itself,
or He is Himself "the way." Works are
not the way, whether these works are legal
or gospel works; whether works of law
or works of faith. Works of faith are a

condition of salvation. But they are not " the way." Faith is not the way. Faith is a condition of entering and abiding in this way, but it is not "the way." Christ is Himself " the way." Faith receives Him to reign in the soul and to be its salvation. But it is Christ Himself who is " the way." The soul is saved by Christ Himself, not by doctrine, not by the Holy Spirit, not by works of any kind, not by faith or love, or by any thing whatever but by Christ Himself. The Holy Spirit reveals and introduces Christ to the soul, and the soul to Christ. He takes of Christ's and shows to us. But He leaves it to Christ to save us. He urges and induces us to accept of Christ, to receive Him by appropriating faith as He reveals Him to us. But Christ is the way. It is his being received by us, that saves the soul. But we must perceive the way. We must enter this way by our own act. We must proceed in this way. We must continue in this way to the end of life and to all eternity as indispensable condition of our salvation. " Whither I go ye know, and the way ye know," said Christ. " Thomas said unto Him, Lord we know not whither thou goest, and how can we know the way?" "Jesus saith unto him, I am the way, and the truth, and the life; no man cometh unto the Father but by me. If ye had known me, ye should have known my Father also, and from henceforth ye know Him and have seen Him. Philip saith unto Him, Lord show us the Father, and it sufficeth us. Jesus saith unto him, Have I been so long time with you, and yet hast thou not known me, Philip? He that hath seen me hath seen the Father, and how sayest thou, show us the Father? Believest thou not that I am in the Father, and the Father in me?" Here Christ so identifies Himself with the Father as to insist that he who had seen one had seen the other. When, therefore, He says, no man cometh to the Father but by

CHRIST THE WAY OF SALVATION. 117

Him, we are to understand that no man
need expect to find the true God else-
where than in Him. The visible Christ
embodied the true Godhead. He is the
way to God, for and because He is the
true God and the eternal life and salvation of the soul. Many seem to understand Christ in this relation as nothing
more than a teacher of a system of mo-
rality by the observance of which we may
be saved. Others regard this relation as
only implying that He is the way in the
sense of making an atonement and thus
rendering it possible for us to be forgiven.
Others still understand this language as
implying not only that Christ made an
atonement and opened up a way of access through his death and mediation to
God, but also that He teaches us the great
truths essential to our salvation. Now
all this, in my apprehension, falls entirely,
and I may say infinitely short of the true
spiritual meaning of Christ and the true
spiritual import of this relation. The

above is implied and included in this relation beyond question, but this is not all
nor the essential truth intended in this
declaration of Christ's. He did not say,
I came to open the way nor to teach the
way, nor to call you into the way, but "*I
am the way.*" Suppose He had intended
merely that his instructions pointed out
the way, or that his death was to open
the way, and his teachings point it out,
would He not have said: What! have
I so long taught you, and have you not
understood my doctrine? Would He not
have said, I have taught you the way,
instead of saying, I am the way? The
fact is, there is meaning in these words,
more profoundly spiritual than his disciples then, and than many now, seem ca-
pable of understanding. He is Himself
the way of salvation, because He is the
salvation of the soul. He is the way to
the Father because He is in the Father
and the Father is in Him. He is the way
to eternal life because He is Himself the

very essence and substance of eternal life. The soul that finds Him needs not to look for eternal life for it has found it already. These questions of Thomas and Philip show how little they really knew of Christ previous to the baptism of the Holy Spirit. Vast multitudes of the professed disciples of the present day, seem not to know Christ as "the way." They seem not to have known Christ in this relation as He is revealed by the Holy Spirit. This revelation by the Comforter, of Christ as "the way," is indispensable to our so knowing Him as to retain our standing in the hour of temptation. We must know and enter and walk and abide in this true and living way for ourselves. It is a living way and not a mere speculation.

Do you, my brother, know Christ by the Holy Spirit as the "living way?" Do you *know Christ* for yourself by a personal acqaintance? or do you know Him only by report, by hearsay, by preaching, by reading and by study? Do you know Him as in the Father and the Father as in Him? Philip seemed not to have had a spiritual and personal revelation of the proper Deity of Christ to his own soul. Have you had this revelation? And when He has been revealed to you as the true and living way, have you by faith personally entered this way? Do you abide steadfast in it? Do you know by experience what it is to live and move and have your very being in God? Be ye not deceived; he that does not spiritually discern and enter this way, and abide in it unto the end, cannot be saved. Do see to it then that you know the way to be sanctified, to be justified, to be saved. See to it that you do not mistake the way and betake yourself to some other way. Remember, works are not the way. Faith is not the way. Doctrine is not the way. All these are conditions of salvation, but *Christ in his own person is "the way."* His own life, living in and united to you is the way and the only way. You enter this way by faith; works of faith result from and are a condition of abiding in this way; but the way itself is the indwelling, living, personally embraced and appropriated Christ: the true God and the eternal life.

Amen, Lord Jesus; the way is pleasant and all its paths are peace.

XXXVII. Christ is also " the Truth," and as such He must be apprehended and embraced to secure the soul from falling in the hour of trial. In this relation many have known Christ merely as one who declared the truth, as one who revealed the true God and the way of salvation. This is all they understand by this assertion of Christ that He is the Truth.

But if this is all, why may not the same with equal truth be said of Moses, and of Paul and John? They taught the truth. They revealed the true God so far as holy lives and true doctrine are concerned; and yet who ever heard of John, or Paul or

6

Moses as being the way and the truth?
They taught the way and the truth, but
they were neither the way nor the truth,
while Christ is truth. What, then, is
truth? Why, Christ is the truth. Whoever knows Christ spiritually, knows the
truth. Words are not the truth. Ideas
are not the truth. But words and ideas
may be signs and representatives of the
truth. But the truth lives and has a being and a home in Christ. He is the
embodiment and essence of truth. He is
reality. He is substance and not shadow.
He is truth revealed. He is elementary,
essential, eternal, immutable, necessary,
absolute, self-existent, infinite Truth.
When the Holy Spirit reveals truth, he
reveals Christ. When Christ reveals
truth, He reveals Himself. Philosophers
have found it difficult to define truth.
Pilate asked Christ, what is truth, but
did not wait for an answer. The term
is doubtless used in a double sense.
Sometimes the mere reflection or repre-

sentation of things in signs, such as words, actions, writings, pictures, and diagrams, etc., is called truth; and this is the popular understanding of it. But all things that exist are only signs, reflections, symbols, representations or types of the Author of all things. That is, the universe is only the objective representation of the subjective truth, or is the reflection or reflector of God. It is the mirror that reflects the essential truth or the true and living God.

But I am aware that none but the Holy Spirit can possess the mind of the import of this assertion of Christ. It is full of mystery and darkness, and is a mere figure of speech to one unenlightened by the Holy Spirit in respect to its true spiritual import. The Holy Spirit does not reveal all the relations of Christ to the soul at once. Hence there are many to whom Christ has been revealed in some of his relations while others are yet veiled from the view. Each distinct name and

office and relation needs to be made the
subject of a special and personal revelation to the soul, to meet its necessities,
and to confirm it in obedience under all
circumstances.   When Christ is revealed
and apprehended as the essential, eternal,
and immutable truth, and the soul has embraced Him as such, as He of whom all
that is popularly called truth is only the
reflection, as He of whom all truth in doctrine, whether of philosophy in any of its
branches, or revelation in any of its de-
partments; I say, when the mind apprehends Him as that essential truth of which
all that men call truth, is only the reflection, it finds a rock, a resting place, a
foundation, a stability, a reality, a power
in truth of which before it had no conception.   If this is unintelligible to you,
I cannot help it.   The Holy Spirit can
explain and make you see it; I cannot.
Christ is not truth in the sense of mere
doctrine, nor in the sense of a teacher of
true doctrine, but as the substance or

essence of truth. He is that of which all truth in doctrine treats. True doctrine treats of Him, but is not identical with Him. Truth in doctrine is only the sign, or declaration, or representation of truth in essence, of living, absolute, self-existent truth in the Godhead. • Truth in doctrine or true doctrine is a medium through which substantial or essential truth is revealed. But the doctrine or medium is no more identical with truth than light is identical with the object which it reveals. Truth in doctrine is called light and is to essential truth what light is to the objects that radiate or reflect it. Light coming from objects, is at once the condition of and the medium through which they are revealed. So true doctrine is the condition and the means of knowing Christ, the essential truth. All truth in doctrine is only a reflection of Christ, or is a radiation upon the intelligence from Christ. When we learn this spiritually, we shall learn to distinguish between doctrine and

Him whose radiance it is—to worship Christ as the essential truth and not the doctrine that reveals Him—to worship God instead of the Bible. We shall then find our way through the shadow to the substance. Many, no doubt, mistake and fall down and worship the doctrine, the preacher, the Bible, the shadow, and do not look for the ineffably glorious substance of which this bright and sparkling truth is only the sweet and mild reflection or radiation.

Dearly beloved, do not mistake the doctrine for the thing treated of by the doctrine. When you find your intellect enlightened and your sensibility quickened by the contemplation of doctrine, do not confound this with Christ. Look steadily in the direction from which the light emanates until the Holy Spirit enables you to apprehend the essential truth, and the true light that enlighteneth every man. Do not mistake a dim reflection of the sun for the sun himself. Do not fall down at a pool and worship the sun dimly reflected from its surface, but lift your eye and see where he stands glorious in essential and eternal and ineffable brightness. It is beyond question that multitudes of professed Christians know nothing farther than the doctrine of Christ; they never had Christ Himself personally revealed or manifested to them. The doctrine of Christ as taught in the gospel is intended to direct and draw the mind to Him. The soul must not rest in the doctrine, but receive the living, essential person and substance of Christ. The doctrine makes us acquainted with the facts concerning Christ, and presents Him for acceptance. Do not rest in the story of Christ crucified and risen and standing at the door, but open the door and receive the risen, living and Divine Savior as the essential and all-powerful truth to dwell within you forever.

XXXVIII. Christ is " the TRUE LIGHT." John says of Him, "In Him was life, and the life was the Light of men. And the Light shineth in darkness and the darkness comprehended it not. There was a man sent from God whose name was John. The same came for a witness to bear witness of the *Light*, that all men through Him might believe. He was not that *Light*, but He came to bear witness of that *Light*. That was the TRUE LIGHT which lighteneth every man that cometh into the world." Jesus says, " I am the light of the world; he that followeth me shall not walk in darkness, but shall have the light of life." And Again, " While ye have the light, believe in the light." " I am come a light into the world." Again, it is said of Saul on his way to Damascus, " And there shined around him a light from heaven, above the brightness of the sun." It is said of Christ in his transfiguration on the mount, " that his raiment became white as the light." Paul speaks of Christ as dwelling in light which no man can approach unto. Peter says of Him, "who called you into his marvellous light." John says, "God is light and in Him is no darkness at all." Of the New Jerusalem it is said, that the inhabitants have no need of the sun, nor of the moon to en-lighten it, " for the glory of God and the Lamb are the light thereof."

Light certainly appears to be of two kinds, as every spiritual mind knows, physical and spiritual. Physical or natural light reveals or makes manifest physical objects through the fleshly organ, the eye. Spiritual light is no less real light than physical. In the presence of spiritual light the mind directly sees spiritual truths and objects, as, in the presence of material or natural light, it distinctly sees material objects. The mind has an eye or seeing faculty which uses the material eye and natural light to discern material objects. It is not the eye that sees. It is always the mind that sees. It uses the eye merely as an instrument of vision by which it discerns material objects. The eye and

6*

the light are conditions of seeing the material universe, but it is always the mind that sees.

So the mind directly sees spiritual realities in the presence of spiritual light. But what is light? What is natural, and what is spiritual light? Are they really identical, or are they essentially different? It is not my purpose here to enter into any philosophical speculations upon this subject; but I must observe, that whatever spiritual light is, the mind under certain circumstances cannot discern the difference, if difference there is between them. Was that spiritual or physical light which the disciples saw on the mount of transfiguration? Was that spiritual or physical light which Paul and his companions saw on their way to Damascus? What light is that which falls upon the mental eye of the believer when he draws so near to God as not at the moment to at all distinguish the glory that surrounds him from material light? What was that

light which made the face of Moses shine
with such brightness that the people
were unable to behold it? And what
is that light which lights up the countenance of a believer when he comes direct
and fresh from the mount of communion
with God? There is often a visible light
in his countenance. What is that light
which often shines upon the pages of the
Bible, making its spiritual meaning as manifest to the mind as the letters and words
are? In such seasons the obscurity is re-
moved from the *spirit* of the Bible, just
as really and as visibly as the rising
sun would remove the obscurity of mid-
night from the *letter.* In one case you
perceive the *letter* clearly in the presence
of natural light. You have no doubt,
you can have no doubt, that you see the
letters and words as they are. In the
other, you apprehend the *spirit* of the
Bible just as clearly as you see the letter.
You can no more doubt at the time that
you see the true spiritual import of the

words, than that you see the words themselves. Both the letter and the spirit seem to be set in so strong a light that you know that you see both. Now what light is this in which the *spirit* of the Bible is seen? That it is light every spiritual man knows. He calls it light. He can call it nothing else. At other times the letter is as distinctly visible as before, and yet there is no possibility of discerning the spirit of the Bible. It is then only known in the letter. We are then left to philologize, and philosophize, and theorize, and theologize, and are really all in the dark as to the true spiritual import of the Bible. But when "the true light that lighteth every man," shines upon the world, we get at once a deeper insight into the real spiritual import of the word than we could have gotten in a life-time without it. Indeed, the true spiritual import of the Bible is hid from the learning of this world, and revealed to the babes who are in the light of Christ. I have often been afflicted with the fact that true spiritual light is rejected and contemned, and the very idea of its existence rejected by many men who are wise in the wisdom of this world. But the Bible every where abounds with evidence that spiritual light exists, and that its presence is a condition of apprehending the reality and presence of spiritual objects. It has been generally supposed that the natural sun is the source of natural light. Sure it is that light is a condition of our beholding the objects of the material universe. But what is the source of spiritual light? The Bible says Christ is. But what does this mean? When it is said that He is the true light, does it mean only that He is the Teacher of true doctrine? Or does it mean that He is the light in which true doctrine is apprehended, or its spiritual import understood; that He shines through and upon all spiritual doctrine, and causes its spiritual import to be apprehended, and that the

presence of his light or in other words his
own presence, is a condition of any doctrines being spiritually understood ?   He
is no doubt the essential light.   That is,
light is an attribute of his Divinity.   Essential, uncreated light is one of the attributes of Christ as God.   It is a spiritual
attribute of course.   But it is an essential
and a natural attribute of Christ, and
whoever knows Christ *after the Spirit*,
or whoever has a true, spiritual, and personal acquaintance with Christ as God,
knows th at Christ is light, that his being
called light is not a mere figure of speech;
that his "covering himself with light as
with a garment;" his enlightening the
heavenly world with so ineffable a light
that no man can approach thereunto and
live, that the strongest seraphim are unable to look with unveiled face upon his
overpowering effulgence :—I say, to a
spiritual mind, these are not mere figures
of speech ; they are understood by those
who are in the light, and who walk

in the light of Christ, to mean what they say.

I dwell upon this particular relation of Christ because of the importance of its being understood, that Christ is the real and true light who alone can cause us to see spiritual things as they are. Without his light we walk in the midst of the most overpowering realities without being at all aware of their presence. Like one surrounded with natural darkness, or as one deprived of natural light gropes his way and knows not at what he stumbles, so one deprived of the presence and light of Christ, gropes his way and stumbles at he knows not what. To attain to true spiritual illumination and to continue and walk in this light, is indispensable to entire sanctification. O that this were understood! Christ must be known as the true and only light of the soul. This must not be held merely as a tenet. It must be understood and spiritually experienced and known. That Christ is in some unde-

termined sense the light of the soul, and
the true light is generally admitted just
as multitudes of other things are admitted
without being at all spiritually and experimentally understood.   But this relation
or attribute of Christ must be spiritually
known by experience as a condition of
abiding in Him.   John says, " this then is
the message which we have heard of Him,
that God is light, and in Him is no darkness at all.   If we say that we have fellowship with Him and walk in darkness,
we lie and do not the truth.   But if we
walk in the light, as He is in the light, we
have fellowship one with another, and the
blood of Jesus Christ his Son cleanseth us
from all sin."   This light is come into the
world, and if men do not love darkness
rather than light, they will know Christ
as the true light of the soul and will so
walk in the light as not to stumble.

I desire much to amplify upon this relation of Christ, but must forbear or I shall
too much enlarge this course of insruc-

tion. I would only endeavor to deeply impress you with the conviction that Christ is light, and that this is no figure of speech. Rest not, my brother, until you truly and experimentally know Him as such. Bathe your soul daily in his light, so that when you come from your closet your face will shine as if it were the face of an angel.

CHAPTER V.

XXXIX. Another relation which Christ sustains to the believer, and which it is indispensable that he should recognize and spiritually apprehend as a condition of entire sanctification, is that of "Christ within us."

" Know ye not," says the apostle, "that Jesus Christ is in you except ye be reprobates."—2 Cor. 13: 5. " But ye are not in the flesh, but in the Spirit if the Spirit of God dwell in you. Now if any man have not the Spirit of Christ, he is none of his. And if Christ be in you, the body is dead because of sin, but the Spirit is life because of righteousness."—Ro. 8: 9, 10. " My

ittle children, of whom I travail in birth
again until Christ be formed in you."—
Gal. 4: 19. " Yet not I, but Christ liveth
in me."—Gal. 2: 20. Now it has often
appeared to me that many know Christ
only as an outward Christ, as one who
lived many hundred years ago, who died,
and arose, and ascended on high, and who
now lives in heaven. They read all this
in the Bible, and in a certain sense they
believe it. That is they admit it to be
true historically. But have they Christ
risen within them? living within the veil
of their own flesh and there ever making
intercession for them and in them? This
is quite another thing. Christ in heaven
making intercession is one thing; this is a
great and glorious truth. But Christ in
the soul, there also living " to make intercession for us with groanings that cannot be uttered," is another thing. The
Spirit that dwells in the saints is frequently
in the Bible represented as the Spirit of
Christ and as Christ himself. Thus in

the passage just quoted from the eighth of Romans, the apostle represents the Spirit of God that dwells in the saints as the Spirit of Christ and as Christ Himself. Rom. 8: 9, 10: "But ye are not in the flesh, but in the Spirit, if so be that the Spirit of God dwell in you. Now if any man have not the Spirit of Christ, he is none of his. And if Christ be in you, the body is dead because of sin; but the spirit is life because of righteousness." This is common in the Bible. The Spirit of Christ then, or the real deity of Christ dwells in the truly spiritual believer. But this fact needs to be spiritually apprehended and kept distinctly and continually in view. Christ not only in heaven, but Christ within us, as really and truly inhabiting our bodies as we do, as really in us as we are in ourselves, is the teaching of the Bible, and must be spiritually apprehended by a divine, personal, and inward revelation, to secure our abiding in Him. We not only need the real presence of

Christ within us, but we need his manifested presence to sustain us in hours of
conflict. Christ may be really present
within us as He is without us, without our
apprehending his presence. His manifesting Himself to us with and in us is by
Himself conditionated upon our faith and
obedience. His manifesting Himself within us and thus assuring us of his constant
and real presence, confirms and establishes the confidence and obedience of the
soul. To know Christ after the flesh or
merely historically as an outward Savior,
is of no spiritual avail. We must know
Him as an inward Savior, as Jesus risen
and reigning in us, as having arisen and
established his throne in our hearts, and
as having written and established the authority of his law there. The old man de-
throned and crucified, Christ risen within
us and united to us in such a sense that we
" twain are one spirit," is the true and
only condition and secret of entire sanctification. O that this were understood

Why, many ministers talk and write about sanctification just as if they supposed that it consisted in and resulted from a mere self-originated formation of holy habits. What infinite blindness this for spiritual guides! True sanctification consists in entire consecration to God; but be it ever remembered that this consecration is induced and perpetuated by the Spirit of Christ. The fact that Christ is in us needs to be so clearly apprehended by us as to annihilate the conception of Christ as only afar off, in heaven. The soul needs so to apprehend this truth as to turn within and not look without for Christ, so that it will naturally seek communion with Him in the closet of the soul, or within, and not let the thoughts go in search of Him without. Christ promised to come and take up his abode with his people, to manifest Himself unto them, etc., that the Spirit whom He would send, (which was his own Spirit as abundantly appears from the Bible,) should abide with them forever, that He should be with them and in them. Now all this language needs to be spiritually apprehended, and Christ needs to be recognized as by his Spirit as really present with us as we are with ourselves, and really as near to us as we are to ourselves, and as infinitely more interested in us than we are in ourselves. This spiritual recognition of Christ present with and in us, has an overpowering charm in it. The soul rests in Him and lives, and walks, and has its being in his light, and drinks at the fountain of his love. It drinks also of the river of his pleasures. It enjoys his peace, and leans upon his strength.

Many professors have not Christ formed within them. The Galatian Christians had fallen from Christ. Hence the apostle says: "My little children of whom I travail in birth again until Christ be formed in you." Have you a spiritual apprehension of what this means?

XL. We must spiritually knows Christ as "*our Strength*," as a condition of entire sanctification. Says the Psalmist, Ps. 18: 1; "I will love thee, O Lord, my strength;" and again, 19: 14; "O Lord my strength;" and again, 31: 4; "Pull me out of the net for Thou art my strength;" and again, 43:2; "Thou art the God of my strength;" and again, 59: 17; "To Thee, O my strength, will I sing;" and again, 144: 1; "Blessed be the Lord my strength." In Is. 27: 5; "The Lord says, Let him take hold of my strength and he shall make peace with me." Jeremiah says, Jer. 16: 19; "O Lord, my strength." Hab. 3: 9: "God is my strength." In 2 Cor. 12: 9, Christ says to Paul, "My strength is made perfect in weakness." We are commanded to be strong in the Lord and in the power of his might, that is, to appropriate his strength by faith. We are exhorted to take hold on his strength, and doing this is made a condition of making peace with

God. That God is in some sense our strength is generally admitted. But I fear it is rare to apprehend the true spiritual sense in which He is our strength. Many take refuge, not in his strength by faith, but in the plea that He is their strength, and that they have none of their own while they continue in sin. But this class of persons neither truly understand nor believe that God is their strength. It is with all who hold this language and yet live in sin, an opinion, a tenet, a sayso, but by no means a spiritually apprehended and embraced truth. If the real meaning of this language were spiritually apprehended and embraced with the heart, the soul would no more live in sin. It would no more be overcome with temptation while appropriating Christ than God would be overcome.

The conditions of spiritually apprehending Christ as our strength, are:

1. The spiritual apprehension of our own weakness, its nature and degree.

7

2. The revelation of Christ to us as our strength by the Holy Spirit.

When these revelations are truly made and self-dependence is therefore forever annihilated, the soul comes to understand wherein its strength lies. It renounces forever its own and relies wholly on the strength of Christ. This it does not in the Antinomian, do-nothing, sit-still sense of the term; but on the contrary it actively takes hold of Christ's strength and uses it in doing all the will of God. It does not sit down and do nothing, but on the contrary it takes hold of Christ's strength and sets about every good word and work as one might lean upon the strength of another and go about doing good. The soul that understands and does this as really holds on to and leans upon Christ as a helpless man would lean upon the arm or shoulder of a strong man to be borne about in some benevolent enterprise. It is not a state of quietism. It is not a mere opinion, a sentiment, a humbug. It is, with the sanctified soul, one of the clearest realities in existence that he leans upon and uses the strength of Christ. He knows himself to be constantly and perseveringly active in thus availing himself of the strength of Christ; and being perfectly weak in himself, or perfectly emptied of his own strength, Christ's strength is made perfect in his weakness. This renunciation of his own strength is not a denial of his natural ability in any such sense as virtually to charge God with requiring what He is unable to perform. It is a complete recognition of his ability were he disposed to do all that God requires of him, and implies a thorough and honest condemnation of himself for not using his powers as God requires. But while it recognizes its natural liberty or ability and its consequent obligation, it at the same time clearly and spiritually sees that it has been too long the slave of lust ever to assert or maintain its spiritual supremacy as the master instead of the slave of appetite. It sees so clearly and affectingly that the will or heart is so weak in the presence of temptation that there is no hope of its maintaining its integrity unsupported by strength from Christ, that it renounces forever its dependence on its own strength, and casts itself wholly and forever on the strength of Christ. Christ's strength is appropriated only upon condition of a full renunciation of one's own. And Christ's strength is made perfect in the soul of man only in its entire weakness; that is, only in the absence of all dependence on its own strength. Self must be renounced in every respect in which we appropriate Christ. He will not share the throne of the heart with us, nor will he be put on by us except in so far forth as we put off ourselves. Lay aside all dependence on yourself in every respect in which you would have Christ. Many reject Christ by depending on self, and seem not to be aware of their error.

Now, do let it be understood and constantly borne in mind that this self-renunciation and taking hold on Christ as our strength is not a mere speculation, an opinion, an article of faith, a profession, but must be one of the most practical realities in the world. It must become to the mind an omnipresent reality in so much that you shall no more attempt any thing in your own strength than a man who never could walk without crutches would attempt to arise and walk without thinking of them. To such an one his crutches become a part of himself. They are his legs. He as naturally uses them as we do the members of our body. He no more forgets them, or attempts to walk without them than we attempt to walk without our feet. Now just so it is with one who spiritually understands his dependence on Christ. He knows he can walk and that he must walk, but he as naturally uses the strength of Christ in all his duties as the lame man uses his crutches.

It is as really an omnipresent reality to him that he must lean upon Christ as it is to the lame man that he must lean upon his crutch. He learns on all occasions to keep hold of the strength of Christ and does not even think of doing any thing without Him. He knows that he need not attempt any thing in his own strength; and if he should, he knows it will result in failure and disgrace just as really and as well as the man without feet or legs knows that for him to attempt to walk without his crutch would insure a fall. This is a great, and, I fear, a rarely learned lesson with professed Christians, and yet how strange that it should be so, since in every instance, since the world began, attempts to walk without Christ have resulted in complete and instantaneous failure. All profess to know their own weakness and their remedy, and yet how few give evidence of knowing either!

XLI. Christ is also the *Keeper* of the soul; and in this relation He must be revealed to and embraced by each soul 'as the condition of its abiding in Christ, or which is the same thing, as a condition of entire sanctification. Ps. 121 : "I will lift up mine eyes unto the hills, from whence cometh my help. My help cometh from the Lord which made heaven and earth. He will not suffer thy foot to be moved ; He that keepeth thee will not slumber. Behold He that keepeth Israel shall neither slumber nor sleep. The Lord is thy keeper; the Lord is thy shade upon thy right hand. The sun shall not smite thee by day, nor the moon by night. The Lord shall preserve thee from all evil ; He shall preserve thy soul. The Lord shall preserve thy going out, and thy coming in, from this time forth, and even forevermore." This Psalm with a· great many other passages of scripture represent God as exerting an efficient influence in preserving the soul from falling. This influence He exerts, of course not physically or by compulsion, but it is and must be moral influence, that is an influence entirely consistent with our own free agency. But it is efficient in the sense of being a prevailing influence.

But in this relation as in all others, Christ must be apprehended and embraced. The soul must see and well appreciate its dependence in this respect, and commit itself to Christ in this relation. It must cease from its own works and from expecting to keep itself and commit itself to Christ and abide in this state of committal. Keeping his soul implies watching over it to guard it against being overcome with temptation. This is exactly what the Christian needs. His enemies are the world, the flesh, and Satan. By these he has been enslaved. To them he has been consecrated. In their presence he is all weakness in himself. He needs a keeper to accompany him, just as a reformed inebriate sometimes needs one to accompany and strengthen him in

scenes of temptation. The long established habits of the drunkard render
him weak in the presence of his enemy,
the intoxicating bowl. So the Christian's
long-cherished habits of self-indulgence
render him all weakness and irresolution
if left to himself in the presence of excited
appetite or passion. As the inebriate
needs a friend and brother to warn and
expostulate, to suggest considerations to
strengthen his purposes, so the sinner
needs the *Paracletus* to warn and suggest
considerations to sustain his fainting resolutions. This Christ has promised to do;
but this, like all the promises, is conditionated upon our appropriating it to our own
use by faith. Let it then be ever borne
in mind that as our keeper, the Lord must
be spiritually apprehended and cordially
embraced and depended upon as a condition of entire sanctification. This must
not be a mere opinion. It must be a
thorough and honest closing in with Christ
in this relation.

Brother, do you know what it is to depend on Christ in this relation in such a sense that you as naturally hold fast to Him as a child would cling to the hand or the neck of a father when in the midst of perceived danger? Have you seen your need of a keeper? If so, have you fled to Christ in this relation? As ye have received Jesus Christ the Lord, so walk ye in Him, that is, abide in Him and He will abide in you and keep you from falling. The apostle certifies, or rather assumes that He is able to keep you from falling. " Now unto Him that is able to keep you from falling, and to present you faultless before the presence of his glory with exceeding joy—to the only wise God our Savior, be glory and majesty, dominion and power, both now and ever, Amen."—Jude 25 : 25. Paul also says: "I knew in whom I have believed, and am persuaded that He is able to keep that which I have committed to Him against that day."

XLII. The soul needs also to know Christ, not merely as a master, but as a *Friend*. John 15: 13—15. "Greater love hath no man than this, that a man lay down his life for his friends. Ye are my friends, if ye do whatsoever I command you. Henceforth I call you not servants, for the servant knoweth not what his Lord doeth; but I have called you friends, for all things that I have heard of my Father I have made known unto you."

Christ took the utmost pains to inspire his disciples with the most implicit confidence in Him. He does the same still. Most Christians seem not to have apprehended the condescension of Christ sufficient to appreciate fully, not to say at all, his most sincere regard for them. They seem afraid to regard Him in the light of a friend, one whom they may approach on all occasions with the utmost confidence and holy familiarity, one who takes a lively interest in every thing that concerns them, one who sympathizes with them in all their trials, and feels more tenderly for them than we do for our nearest earthly friends.   Observe, what emphasis He gives to this relation or to the strength of his friendship.   He lays down his life for his friends.   Now imagine yourself to have an earthly friend who loved you so much as to lay down his life for you; to die, too, for a crime which you had committed against himself.   Were you assured of the strength of his friendship, and did you know withal his ability to help you in all circumstances to be absolutely unlimited, with what confidence would you unbosom yourself to Him?   How would you rest in his friendship and protection?   Now even Christians are slow to apprehend Christ in the relation of a *friend*.   They stand in so much awe of Him that they fear to take home to their hearts the full import and reality of the relation when applied to Christ.   Yet Christ takes the greatest pains to inspire them with the fullest confidence in his undying and most exalted friendship.

I have often thought that many professed Christians had never really and spiritually apprehended Christ in this relation. This accounts for their depending upon Him so little in seasons of trial. They do not realize that He truly feels for and sympathizes with them; that is, his feeling for and sympathy with them, his deep interest in and pity for them, are not apprehended spiritually, as a reality Hence they stand aloof or approach Him only in words, or at most with deep feeling and desire, but not in the unwavering confidence that they shall receive the things which they ask of Him. But to prevail, they must believe. " Let not that man that wavereth, think to receive any thing of the Lord." The real, and deep, and abiding affection of Christ for us, and his undying interest in us personally, must come to be a living and an omnipresent reality to our souls, to secure

our own abiding in faith and love in al.
circumstances. There is, perhaps, no relation of Christ in which we need more
thoroughly to know Him than this.

This relation is admitted in words by
almost everybody, yet duly realized and
believed by almost nobody. Yet how infinitely strange that Christ should have
given so high evidence of his love to, and
friendship for us, and that we should be
so slow of heart to believe and realize it!
But until this truth is really and spiritually
apprehended and embraced, the soul will
find it impossible to fly to Him in seasons of trial with implicit confidence in
his favor and protection. But let Christ
be really apprehended and embraced as a
friend who has laid down his life for us,
and who would not hesitate to do it again,
were it needful—and rely upon it, our
confidence in Him will secure our abiding
in Him.

XLIII. Christ is also to be regarded and
embraced in the relation of an Elder

Brother: Heb. 2: 10—18: "For it became Him, for whom are all things, and by whom are all things, in bringing many sons unto glory, to make the Captain of their salvation perfect through sufferings. For both He that sanctifieth, and they who are sanctified are all of one: for which cause He is not ashamed to call them brethren: saying, I will declare thy name unto my brethren: in the midst of the church will I sing praise unto thee. And again, I will put my trust in Him. And again, Behold I and the children which God hath given me. Forasmuch then, as the children are partakers of flesh and blood, He also Himself likewise took part of the same: that through death He might destroy him that had the power of death, that is, the devil; and deliver them who through fear of death were all their life-time subject to bondage. For verily, He took not on Him the nature of angels; but He took on Him the seed of Abraham. Wherefore in all things it behoved Him to

be made like unto his brethren, that He
might be a merciful and faithful high priest
in things pertaining to God, to make reconciliation for the sins of the people: for
in that He Himself hath suffered, being
tempted, He is able to succor them that
are tempted." Matt. 28: 10; " Then
said Jesus unto them, Be not afraid : go
tell my brethren, that they go into Galilee,
and there shall they see me."　John 20:
17; " Jesus saith unto her, Touch me
not ; for 1 am not yet ascended to my
Father ; but go to my brethren, and say
unto them, I ascend unto my Father, and
your Father; and to my God and your
God."　Rom. 8: 29; "For whom He did
foreknow, He also did predestinate to be
conformed to the image of his 'Son, that
He might be the first-born among many
brethren."　These and other passages
present Christ in the relation of a brother.
So He is not merely a friend, but a brother.
He is a brother possessing the attributes
of God.　And it is not of great impor-

tance that in this relation we should know and embrace Him. It would seem as if all possible pains were taken by Him to inspire us with the most implicit confidence in Him. He is not ashamed to call us brethren; and shall we refuse or neglect to embrace Him in this relation, and avail ourselves of all that is implied in it? I have often thought that many professed Christians really regard the relations of Christ as only existing in name and not at all in reality and fact. Am I not a man and a brother? He says to the desponding and tempted soul. Himself hath said, A brother is made for adversity. He is the first-born among many brethren, and yet we are to be heirs with Him, heirs of God and joint heirs with Him to all the infinite riches of the Godhead. "O fools and slow of heart," not to believe and receive this brother to our most implicit and eternal confidence. He must be spiritually revealed, apprehended and embraced in this relation as a condition

of our experiencing his fraternal truthfulness.

Do let me inquire whether many Christians do not regard such language as pa-
thetic and touching, but after all as only
a figure of speech, as a pretense, rather
than as a serious and infinitely important
fact. Is the Father really our Father?
Then Christ is our brother, not in a figura-
tive sense, merely, but literally and truly
our brother. My brother? Ah, truly,
and a brother made for adversity. O!
Lord, reveal thyself fully to our souls in
this relation.

XLIV. Christ is the True Vine and we
are the branches. And do we know Him
in this relation, as our parent stock, as the
fountain from whom we receive our mo-
mentary nourishment and life? This
union between Christ and our souls is
formed by implicit faith in Him. By faith
the soul leans on Him, feeds upon Him,
and receives a constantly sustaining influence from Him. John 15: 1—8; "I

ιm the True Vine, and my Father is the Husbandman. Every branch in me that ɔeareth not fruit He taketh away; and ɛvery branch that beareth fruit, He purgɛth it that it may bring forth more fruit. Now ye are clean through the word which I have spoken unto you. Abide in me and I in you. As the branch cannot bear fruit of itself except it abide in the vine; no more can ye, except ye abide in me. I am the Vine, ye are the branches; he that abideth in me, and I in him, the same bringeth forth much fruit; for without me ye can do nothing. If a man abide not in me, he is cast forth as a branch, and is withered ; and men gather them, and cast them into the fire, and they are burned. If ye abide in me, and my words abide in you, ye shall ask what ye will, and it shall be done unto you. Herein is my Father glorified, that ye bear much fruit, so shall ye be my disciples." Now it is important for us to understand what it is to be in Christ in the

sense of this passage. It certainly is to
be so united to Him as to receive as real
and as constant spiritual support and nourishment from Him as the branch does natural nourishment from the vine. "If a
man abide not in me," He says, "he is
cast forth as a branch and is withered."
Now to be in Him implies such a union
as to keep us spiritually alive and fresh.
There are many withered professors in the
church. They abide not in Christ. Their
religion is stale. They can speak of former experience. They can tell how they
once knew Christ, but every spiritual
mind can see that they are branches fallen
off. They have no fruit. Their leaves
are withered, their bark is dried; and
they are just fit to be gathered and cast
into the fire. O this stale, last year's religion! Why will not professors that live
on an old experience, understand that
they are cast off branches, and that their
withered, fruitless, lifeless, loveless, faith-
less, powerless condition testifies to their

faces and before all men that they are fit for the flames.

It is also of infinite importance that we should know and spiritually apprehend the conditions of abiding in Christ in the relation of a branch to a vine. We must apprehend our various necessities and his infinite fullness, and lay hold upon and appropriate the whole that is implied in these relations to our own souls and wants as fast as He is revealed. Thus we shall abide in Him and receive all the spiritual nourishment we need. But unless we are thus taught by the Spirit, and unless we thus believe, we shall not abide in Him nor He in us. If we do thus abide in Him, He says we shall bear much fruit. Much fruit, then, is evidence that we do abide in Him, and fruitlessness is positive evidence that we do not abide in Him. " If ye abide in me, and my words abide in you, ye shall ask what ye will and it shall be done unto you." Great prevalence in prayer, then, is an evidence that we abide in Him. But a want of prevalence in prayer is conclusive evidence that we do not abide in Him. No man sins while he properly abides in Christ. "If any man be in Christ, he is a new creature. Old things are passed away, and behold all things are become new."

But let it not be forgotten that we have someting to do to abide in Christ.— "Abide in me," says Christ: this is required of us. We neither at first come to sustain the relation of a branch to Christ without our own activity, nor do or can we abide in Him without a constant cleaving to Him by faith. The will must of necessity be ever alive. It must cleave to Christ or to something else. It is one thing to hold this relation in theory, and an infinitely different thing to understand it spiritually and really cleave to Christ in the relation of the constant fountain of spiritual life.

XLV. Christ is also the "Fountain opened in the house of David for sin and uncleanness;" Zec. 13; 1. Christ, (let it be ever remembered, and spiritually understood and embraced,) is not only a justifying, but also a purifying Savior. His name is Jesus, because He saves his people from their sins.

XLVI. As Jesus, therefore, He must be spiritually known and embraced. Jesus, Savior! He is called Jesus or Savior we are informed, because He saves his people, not only from hell, but also from their sins. He saves from hell only upon condition of his saving from sin. He has no Savior, who is not in his own experience saved from sin. Of what use is it to call Jesus Lord and Savior unless He is really and practically acknowledged as our Lord and as our Savior from sin. Shall we call Him Lord, Lord, and do not the things which He says? Shall we call Him Savior, and refuse to so embrace Him as to be saved from our sins?

XLVII. We must know Him as one whose blood cleanses us from all sin.

Heb. 9: 14; "How much more shall the blood of Christ, who through the eternal Spirit offered Himself without spot to God, purge your conscience from dead works to serve the living God?" 1 Peter 1: 19; "But with the precious blood of Christ, as of a lamb without blemish and without spot." 1 Peter 1: 2; "Elect according to the foreknowledge of God the Father, through sanctification of the Spirit, unto obedience and sprinkling of the blood of Jesus Christ." Rev. 1: 5; "Unto Him that loved us, and washed us from our sins in his own blood." When the shedding of Christ's blood is rightly apprehended and embraced, when his atonement is properly understood and received by faith, it cleanses the soul from all sin: or rather, I should say, that when Christ is received as one to cleanse us from sin by his blood, we shall know what James B. Taylor meant when he said, "I have been into the fountain and am clean," and what Christ meant when He said "Now ye are clean through the word which I have spoken unto you." " Who hath loved us and washed us from our sins in his own blood." "Then will I sprinkle clean water upon you and ye shall be clean, from all your filthiness and from all your idols will I cleanse you. A new heart also will I give you and a new spirit will I put within you. I will take away the stony heart out of your flesh, and give you a heart of flesh." It is of the last importance that language like this, relating to our being cleansed from sin by Christ should be elucidated to our souls by the Holy Spirit, and embraced by faith, and Christ truly revealed in this relation. Nothing but this can save us from sin. But this will fully and effectually do the work. It will cleanse us from *all sin.* It will clease us from *all* our filthiness and from all our idols. It will make us "CLEAN."

XLVIII. "His name shall be called *Wonderful.*" No inward or audible ex-

8

clamation is more common to me of late years than the term Wonderful. When contemplating the nature, the character, the offices, the relations, the salvation of Christ, I find [myself often mentally, and frequently audibly exclaiming WONDERFUL. My soul is filled with wonder, love and praise, as I am led by the Holy Spirit to apprehend Christ sometimes in one and sometimes in another relation as circumstances and trials develop the need I have of Him. I am more and more "astonished at the doctrine of the Lord," and at the Lord Himself from year to year. I have come to the conclusion that there is no end to this either in time or in eternity. He will no doubt to all eternity continue to make discoveries of Himself to his intelligent creatures that shall cause them to exclaim, "WONDERFUL." I find my wonder more and more excited from one stage of Christian experience to another. Christ is indeed wonderful contemplated in every point of view, as God, as man, as God-man, Mediator. Indeed I hardly know in which of his many relations He appears most wonderful when in that relation He is revealed by the Spirit. All, all, is wonderful when He stands revealed to the soul in any of his relations. The soul needs to be so acquainted with Him as to excite and constantly keep awake its wonder and adoration. Contemplate Christ in any point of view and the wonder of the soul is excited. Look at any feature of his character, at any department of the plan of salvation, at any part that He takes in the glorious work of man's redemption, look steadfastly at Him as He is revealed through the gospel by the Holy Spirit at any time and place, in any of his works or ways—and the soul will instantly exclaim WONDERFUL! Yes, He shall be called Wonderful!

XLIX. " *Counsellor.*" Who that has made Jesus his wisdom, does not and has not often recognized the fitness of calling Him " *counsellor?*" Until He is known and

embraced in this relation, it is not natural
or possible for the soul to go to Him with
implicit confidence in every case of doubt,
Almost every body holds in theory the
propriety and necessity of consulting
Christ in respect to the affairs that concern ourselves and his church. But it is
one thing to hold this opinion, and quite
another to so spiritually apprehend and
embrace Christ in the relation of counsellor as naturally to call Him counsellor
when approaching Him in secret, and as
naturally to turn and consult Him on all
occasions, and in respect to every thing
that concerns us; and to consult him too
with implicit confidence in his ability and
willingness to give us the direction we
need. Thoroughly and spiritually to
know Christ in this relation is undoubt-
edly a condition of abiding steadfast in
Him. Unless the soul knows and duly ap-
preciates its dependence upon Him in this
relation, and unless it renounces its own
wisdom and substitutes his in the place of

It, by laying hold of Christ by faith as the counsellor of the soul, it will not continue to walk in his counsel, and consequently will not abide in his love.

L. The Mighty God. " My Lord and my God," exclaimed Thomas when Christ stood spiritually revealed to him. It was not merely what Christ said to Thomas on that occasion that caused him to utter the exclamation just quoted. Thomas saw indeed that Christ was raised from the dead. The mere fact, therefore, that Christ stood before him as one raised from the dead, could not have been proof that He was God. No doubt the Holy Spirit discovered to Thomas at the moment, the true Divinity of Christ, just as the saints in all ages have had Him spiritually revealed to them as the Mighty God. I have long been convinced that it is in vain, so far forth as any spiritual benefit is concerned, to attempt to convince Unitarians of the proper Divinity of Christ. The scriptures are as plain as they can be upon this subject, and yet it is true that no man can say that Jesus is the Lord but by the Holy Spirit. As I have said in substance often, the personal revelation of Christ to the inward man by the Holy Spirit, is a condition of his being known as the "Mighty God." What is Christ to one who does not know Him as God? To such a soul He cannot be a Savior. It is impossible that the soul should intelligently and without idolatry commit it to Him as a Savior unless it knows Him to be the true God. It cannot innocently pray to Him nor worship Him, nor commit the soul to his keeping and protection until it knows Him as the Mighty God. To be orthodox merely in theory, in opinion, is nothing to the purpose of salvation. The soul must *know* Christ as God—must believe in or receive Him as such. To receive Him as any thing else is an infinitely different thing from coming and submitting to Him as the true and living and mighty God.

CHAPTER VI.

LI. Christ is our *Shield*. By this name or in this relation He has always been known to the saints. God said to Abraham, I am thy *Shield*—Gen. 15: 1. Ps. 33: 20; The Lord is my shield. Prov. 30: 5; He is a shield to them that put their trust in Him. A shield is a piece of defensive armor used in war. It is a broad plate made of wood or metal, and borne upon the arm and hand, and in conflict presented between the body and the enemy to protect it against his arrows or his blows. God is the Christian's shield in the spiritual warfare. This is a most interesting and important relation. He who does not know

Christ in this relation, and has not embraced and put Him on as one would buckle on a shield, is all exposed to the assaults of the enemy and will surely be wounded if not slain by his fiery darts. This is more than a figure of speech. No fact or reality is of more importance to the Christian than to know how to hide himself behind and in Christ in the hour of conflict. Unless the Christian has on his shield and knows how to use it he will surely fall in battle. When Satan appears, the soul must present its shield, must take refuge behind and in Christ, or all will be defeat and disgrace. When faith presents Christ as the shield, Satan retires vanquished from the field in every instance. Christ always makes way for our escape, and never did a soul get wounded in conflict who made the proper use of this shield. But Christ needs to be known as our protection, as ready on all occasions to shield us from the curse of the law and from the artillery of the enemy of our souls. Be sure to truly know Him and put Him on in this relation, and then you may always sing of victory.

LII. The Lord is " *The Portion*" of his people.

"I am thy shield and thy exceeding great reward," said God to Abraham. As the reward or portion of the soul we need to know and embrace Christ, as the condition of abiding in Him. We need to know Him as "our exceeding great portion," a present, all-satisfying portion. Unless we so know Christ, as to be satisfied with Him, as all we can ask or desire, we shall not of course abstain from all forbidden sources of enjoyment. Nothing is more indispensable to our entire sanctification than to apprehend the fullness there is in Christ in this relation. When the soul finds in Him all its desires and all its wants fully met, when it sees in Him all that it can conceive of as excellent and desirable, and that He is its portion, it remains at rest. It has little

8*

temptation to go after other lovers or after other sources of enjoyment. It is full. It has enough. It has an infinitely rich and glorious inheritance. What more can it ask or think? The soul that understands what it is to have Christ as its portion, knows that He is an infinite portion, that eternity can never exhaust or even diminish it in the least degree; that the mind shall to all eternity increase in the capacity of enjoying this portion, but that no increase of capacity and enjoyment can diminish aught of the infinite fullness of the *Divine Portion of our souls.*

LIII. Christ is our hope. 1 Tim. 1 : 1; "Paul, an apostle of Jesus Christ by the commandment of God our Savior, and Lord Jesus Christ, which is our Hope." Col. 1 : 26; "To whom God would make known what is the riches of the glory of this mystery among the Gentiles; which is Christ in you the Hope of glory." Our only rational expectation is from Him.

Christ in us is our hope of glory. Without Christ in us we have no good or well-grounded hope of glory. Christ in the gospel, Christ on the cross, Christ risen, Christ in heaven is not our hope; but Christ *in us*, Christ actually present, living and reigning in us as really as He lives and reigns in glory, is our only well-grounded hope. We cannot be too certain of this, for unless we despair of salvation in ourselves or in any other, we do not truly make Christ our hope. The soul that does not know and spiritually know Christ in this relation has no well-grounded hope. He may hope that he is a Christian. 'He may hope that his sins are forgiven—that he shall be saved. But he can have no good hope of glory. It cannot be too fully understood or too deeply realized that absolute despair of help and salvation in any other possible way except by Christ *in us*, is an unalterable condition of our knowing and embracing Christ as our hope. Many

seem to have conceived of Christ as
their hope only in his outward relation, that is, as an atoning Savior, as a
risen and ascended Savior. But the indispensable necessity of having Christ
within them, ruling in their hearts and
establishing his government over their
whole being, is a condition of salvation
of which they have not thought. Christ
cannot be truly and savingly our hope
any farther than He is received into
and reigns in our souls. To hope in
merely an outward Christ, is to hope
in vain. To hope in Christ with true
Christian hope implies, .

1. The ripe and spiritual apprehension
of our hopeless condition without Him.
It implies such an apprehension of our
sins and governmental relations as to
annihilate all hope of salvation upon legal
grounds.

2. Such a perception of our spiritual
bondage to sin, as annihilates all hope
of salvation without his constant influ-

ence and strength to keep us from sin.

3. Such a knowledge of our circumstances of temptation as to empty us of all expectation of fighting our own battles, or of in the least degree making headway against our spiritual foes in our own wisdom and strength.

4. A complete annihilation of all hope from any other source.

5. The revelation of Christ to our souls as our hope by the Holy Spirit.

6. The apprehension of Him as one to dwell in us and to be received by faith to the supreme control of our souls.

7. The hearty and joyful reception of Him in this relation. The dethroning of self or the utter denial or rejection of self and the enthroning and crowning of Christ in the inner man. When Christ is clearly seen to be the only hope of the soul, and when He is spiritually received in this relation, the soul learns habitually and constantly to lean upon Him, to rest in Him, and make no efforts without Him.

LIV. Christ is also our Salvation. Ex.
15 : 3 ; "The Lord is my strength and
song, and He has become my salvation ;
He is my God, and I will prepare Him an
habitation ; my father's God, and I will
exalt Him."   Ps. 27 : 1 ; "The Lord is
my light and my salvation ; whom shall
I fear? the Lord is the strength of my
life ; of whom shall I be afraid?"   Ps.
38 : 22 ; "Make haste to help me, O Lord
my salvation."   Ps. 62 : 7 ; "In God is
my salvation and my glory ; the rock of
my strength, and my refuge, is in God."
Ps. 114 : "The Lord is my strength and
song, and is become my salvation ;" Is.
12 : 2 ; "Behold God is my salvation; I will
trust and not be afraid ; for the Lord Je-
hovah is my strength and my song ; He
also is become my salvation."   Isa. 49 :
6 ; "And he said, It is a light thing that
thou shouldest be my servant, to raise up
the tribes of Jacob, and to restore the
preserved of Israel ; I will also give thee
for a light to the Gentiles, that thou

mayest be my salvation unto the ends of
the earth." Luke 2: 30; "For mine
eyes have seen thy salvation." These
and multitudes of similar passages present
Christ not only as our Savior, but as our
Salvation. That is, He saves us by becoming Himself our salvation. Becoming
our salvation includes and implies the following things:

1. Atonement for our sins.

2. Convincing us of and converting us
from our sins.

3. Sanctifying our souls.

4. Justifying or pardoning and accepting or receiving us to favor.

5. Giving us eternal life and happiness.

6. The bestowment of Himself upon us
as the portion of our souls.

7. The everlasting union of our souls
with God.

All this Christ is to us, and well He
may be regarded, not only as our Savior,
but as our *Salvation.*

Nothing is or can be more important than for us to apprehend Christ in the fullness of his relations to us. Many seem to have but extremely superficial apprehensions of Christ. They seem in a great measure blind to the length, and breadth, and height, and depth of their infinite necessities. Hence they have never sought for such a remedy as is found in Christ. The great mass of Christian professors seem to conceive of the salvation of Christ as consisting in a state of mind resulting not from a real union of the soul with Christ, but resulting merely from understanding and believing the doctrines of Christ. The doctrine of Christ as taught in the Bible was designed to gain for Christ a personal reception to dwell within and rule over us. He that truly believes the gospel, will receive Christ as He is presented in the gospel, that is, for what He is there asserted to be to his people, in all the relations He sustains to our souls, as fast as these relations are revealed to him by the Holy Spirit.

The newly converted soul knows Christ in but few relations. He needs trials and experience to develop his weakness, and to reveal to him his multiplied necessities, and thus lead him to a fuller knowledge of Christ. The new convert embraces Christ so far as he knows him, but at first he knows but little of his need of Him, except in his governmental relations. Subsequent experience is a condition of his knowing Christ in all his fullness. Nor can he be effectually taught the fullness there is in Christ any faster than his trials develop his real necessities. If he embraces all he understands of Christ, this is the whole of present duty in respect to him; but as trials are in his way he will learn more of his own necessities, and must learn more of Christ and appropriate Him in new relations, or he will surely fall.

LV. Christ is also the Rock of our Salvation:

Ps. 19: 14. Let the words of my mouth, and the meditation of my heart, be acceptable in thy sight, O Lord, my strength, [margin, *Rock,*] and my Redeemer.

28 : 1. Unto Thee will I cry, O Lord, my Rock; be not silent to me; lest if Thou be silent to me, I become like them that go down into the pit.

31 : 2. Bow down thine ear to me, deliver me speedily, be thou my strong Rock, for a house of defense to save me. **3.** For thou art my Rock and my fortress; therefore, for thy name's sake, lead me, and guide me.

42: 9. I will say unto God my Rock, why hast thou forgotten me? why go I mourning because of the oppression of the enemy?

61 : 2. From the end of the earth will I cry unto Thee, when my heart is overwhelmed; lead me to the Rock that is higher than I.

73: 26. My flesh and my heart faileth: but God is the strength [margin,

Rock] of my heart, and my portion forever.

78: 35. And they remembered that
God was their Rock, and the high God
their Redeemer.

89: 26. He shall cry unto me, Thou
art my Father, my God, and the Rock of
my salvation.

94: 22. But the Lord is my defense,
and my God is the Rock of my refuge.

95: 1. O come, let us sing unto the
Lord; let us make a joyful noise to the
Rock of our salvation.

Isa. 17: 10. Because thou hast forgotten the God of thy salvation, and hast
not been mindful of the Rock of thy
strength, therefore shalt thou plant pleasant plants, and shalt set it with strange
slips.

32: 2. And a man shall be as a hiding-
place from the wind, and a covert from
the tempest; as rivers of water in a dry
place, as the shadow of a great Rock in a
weary land.

It is deeply interesting and affecting to contemplate the relations in which Christ revealed Himself to the Old Testament saints. He is a Rock of Salvation, a Strong Hold or Place of Refuge. In this relation the soul must know Him, and must take hold of Him or take shelter in Him.

LVI. He is also a Rock Cleft, from which the waters of life flow. 1. Cor. 10 : 14. "And did all drink the same spiritual drink, for they drank of that spiritual Rock that followed them, and that Rock was Christ." As such the soul must know and embrace Him.

LVII. He is a great Rock that is higher than we, rising amid the burning sands of our pilgrimage, under the cooling shadow of which the soul can find repose and comfort. He is like the shadow of a great Rock in a weary land. To apprehend Christ in this relation, the soul needs to be brought into sharp and protracted trials until it is faint and ready to sink in discouragement. When the struggle is too

severe for longer endurance, and the soul
is on the point of giving up in despair,
then when Christ is revealed as a great
rock, standing for its defense against the
heart of its trials, and throwing over it the
cooling, soothing influence of his protection, it finds itself at rest and refreshed,
and readily adopts the language of a nu-
merous class of passages of scripture, and
finds itself to have apprehended Christ as
inspired men apprehended and embraced
Him. It is truly remarkable that in all
our experiences we can find that inspired
writers have had the like, and in every
trial and in every deliverance, in every
new discovery of our emptiness, and of
Christ's fullness, we find the language of
our hearts most fully and aptly expressed
in the language of the living oracles. We
readily discover that inspired men had
fallen into like trials, had Christ revealed
to them in the same relations, and had
similar exercises of mind; insomuch that
no language of our own can so readily

express all that we think and feel and
see.

LVIII. He is the Rock from which the
soul is satisfied with honey. Ps. 81 : 16.
" He should have fed them also with the
finest of wheat; and with honey out of
the rock should I have satisfied thee."
The spiritual mind apprehends this language spiritually, and it is doubtless really.
intended to be understood. It knows
what it is to be satisfied with honey from
the Rock, Christ. The divine sweetness
that often refreshes the spiritual mind
when it betakes itself to the Rock, Christ,
reminds it of the words of this passage of
scripture.

LIX. He is the Rock or Foundation
upon which the church as the temple of
the living God, is builded.

Matt. 16: 18. And I say also unto
thee, That thou art Peter, and upon
this Rock I will build my church—
and the gates of hell shall not prevail
against it.

Rom. 9: 33. As it is written, Behold I lay in Zion a stumbling stone, and a rock of offense; and whosoever believeth on Him shall not be ashamed.

1 Pet. 2: 8. And a stone of stumbling, and a rock of offense, even to them which stumble at the word, being disobedient, whereunto also they were appointed.

He is a sure foundation. He is an eternal Rock, or the Rock of Ages—the corner stone of the whole spiritual edifice. But we must build for ourselves upon this Rock. It is not enough to understand as a tenet, a theory, an opinion, an article of our creed, that Christ is the Rock in this sense. We must see that we do not build upon the sand. Matt. 7: 26, 27. "And every one that heareth these sayings of mine and doeth them not, shall be likened unto a foolish man, which built his house upon the sand; And the rain descended, and the floods came, and beat upon that house ; and it fell and great was the fall of it."

LX. He is the "strength of our heart." He is not only our refuge and strength in our conflicts with outward temptations and trials in the sense expressed in Ps. 46: 1. "God is our refuge and strength, a very present help in trouble," but He is also the strength of our heart and our portion forever, in the sense of Ps. 73: 26; "My flesh and my heart faileth ; but God is the strength of my heart and my portion forever." He braces up and confirms the whole inner man in the way of holiness. What Christian has not at times found himself ready to halt and faint by the way? Temptation seems to steal upon him like a charm. He finds his spiritual strength very low, his resolution weak, and he feels as if he should give way to the slightest temptation. He is afraid to expose himself out of his closet, or even to remain within it lest he should sin. He says with David, "I shall fall by the hand of Saul." He finds himself empty — all weakness and trembling. Were it not that the strength of his heart interposes in time, he would doubtless realize in his experience his worst fears. But who that knows Christ has not often experienced his faithfulness under such circumstances, and felt an immortal awaking, reviving, and strength taking possession of his whole being? What spiritual minister has not often dragged himself into the pulpit so discouraged and faint as to be hardly able to stand, or to hold up his head? He is so weak that his spiritual knees smite one against the other. He is truly empty and feels as if he could not open his mouth. He sees himself to be an empty vine, an empty vessel, a poor, helpless, strengthless infant, lying in the dust before the Lord, unable to stand, or go, or preach, or pray, or do the least thing for Christ. But lo! at this juncture, his spiritual strength is renewed. Christ, the strength of his heart develops his own almightiness within him. His mouth is open. He is strong in faith, giving glory to God. He is made at once a sharp threshing instrument to beat down the mountains of opposition to Christ and his gospel. His bow is renewed in his hand and abides in strength. His mouth is opened and Christ has filled it with arguments. Christ has girded him to the battle, and made strong the arms of his hands with the strength of the mighty God of Jacob.

The same is true of every Christian in substance. He has his seasons of being empty that he may feel his dependence; and anon he is girded with strength from on high, and an immortal and supethuman strength takes possession of his soul. The enemy gives way before him. In Christ he can run through a troop, and in his strength he can leap over a wall. Every difficulty gives way before him, and he is conscious that Christ has strengthened him with strength in his soul. The will seems to have the utmost decision, so that temptation gets an exphatic *no!* without a moment's parley.

LXI. Christ is He through whom we may reckon ourselves dead indeed unto sin, and alive untó God. This we are exhorted and commanded to do. That is, we may and ought to account or reckon ourselves through Him as dead unto sin and alive unto God. But what is implied in this liberty to reckon ourselves dead unto sin and alive unto God through Jesus Christ our Lord? Why, certainly:

1. That through and in Him we have all the provision we need, to keep us from sin.

2. That we may and ought to expect to live without sin.

3. That we ought to account ourselves as having nothing more to do with sin than a dead man has with the affairs of this world.

4. That we may and ought to lay hold on Christ for this full and present death unto sin, and life unto God.

5. That if we do thus reckon ourselves dead unto' sin and alive unto God in the true spiritual sense of this text, we shall find Christ unto our souls all we expect of Him in this relation. If Christ cannot or will not save us from sin, upon condition of our laying hold of Him and reckoning ourselves dead unto sin, and alive unto God through Him, what right had the apostle to say, Reckon yourselves indeed dead unto sin and alive unto God through Jesus Christ our Lord? What! does the apostle tell us to account or reckon ourselves dead indeed unto sin, and shall D. D's tell us that such reckoning or expectation is a dangerous delusion?

Now, certainly nothing less can be meant by reckoning ourselves dead unto sin and alive unto God through Jesus Christ, than that through Christ we should expect to live without sin. And not to expect to live without sin, through Christ, is unbelief. It is a rejec-

tion of Christ in this relation. Through
Christ we ought to expect to live to
God, as much as we expect to live at
all. He that does not expect this, rejects Christ as his sanctification and as
Jesus who saves his people from their
sins.

Do not understand me as teaching
that we must *first* know Christ in all
these relations before we can be sanctified. The thing intended is, that coming
to know Christ in these relations is a condition or the indispensable means of our
steadfastness, or *perseverance* in holiness
under temptation—that when we are
tempted from time to time, nothing can
secure us against a fall but the revelation
of Christ to the soul in these relations
one after another, and our appropriation
of Him to ourselves by faith. The gospel has directly promised in every temptation to open a way of escape so that
we shall be able to bear it. The spirit of
this promise pledges to us such a revela-

tion of Christ as to secure our standing, if we will lay hold upon Him by faith, as revealed. Our circumstances of temptation render it necessary that one time we should apprehend Christ in one relation, and at another time in another. For example, at one time we are tempted to despair by Satan's accusing us of sin, and suggesting that our sins are too great to be forgiven. In this case we need a revelation and an appropriation of Christ as having been made sin for us; that is, as having atoned for our sins—as being our justification or righteousness. This will sustain the soul's confidence and preserve its peace.

At another time we are tempted to despair of overcoming our tendencies to sin and give up our sanctification as a hopeless thing. Now we need a revelation of Christ as our sanctification, etc.

At another time the soul is harrassed with the view of the subtlety and sagacity of its spiritual enemies, and greatly tempted to despair on that account. Now it needs to know Christ as its wisdom.

Again, it is tempted to discouragement on account of the great number and strength of its adversaries. On such occasions, it needs Christ revealed as the Mighty God, as its strong tower, as its hiding place, its munition of Rocks.

Again, the soul is pressed with a sense of the infinite holiness of God, and the infinite distance there is between us and God on account of our sinfulness and his infinite holiness, and on account of his infinite abhorrence of sin and sinners. Now the soul needs to know Christ as its righteousness, and as a Mediator between God and man.

Again, the Christian's mouth is closed with a sense of guilt, so that he cannot look up nor speak to God of pardon and acceptance. He trembles and is confounded before God. He lies along on his face, and despairing thoughts roll a tide of agony through his soul. He is speechless and can only groan out his self-accusations before the Lord. Now as a condition of rising above this temptation to despair, he needs a revelation of Christ as his Advocate, as his High Priest, as ever living to make intercession for him. This view of Christ will enable the soul to commit all to Him in this relation, and maintain its peace and hold on to its steadfastness.

Again, the soul is led to tremble in view of its constant exposedness to besetments on every side, oppressed with such a sense of its own utter helplessness in the presence of its enemies as almost to despair. Now it needs to know Christ as the Good Shepherd who keeps a constant watch over the sheep, and carries the lambs in his bosom. He needs to know Him as a Watchman and a Keeper.

Again it is oppressed with a sense of its own utter emptiness, and is forced to exclaim, I know that in me, that is, in my flesh, dwelleth no good thing. It sees that it has no life, or unction, or power, or spirituality in itself. Now it needs to know Christ as the True Vine from which it may receive constant and abundant spiritual nourishment. It needs to know Him as the fountain of the water of life, and in those relations that will meet its necessities in this direction. Let these suffice as specimens to illustrate what is intended by entire or permanent sanctification being conditioned on revelation and appropriation of Christ in all the fullness of his official relations.

In my estimation, the church as *a body*, I mean the nominal church, have entirely mistaken the nature and means or conditions of sanctification. They have not regarded it as consisting in a state of entire consecration, nor understood that continual entire consecration was entire sanctification. They have regarded sanctification as consisting in the *annihilation* of the constitutional propensities instead of

9*

the controlling of them. They have erred equally in regard to the means or condition of entire sanctification. They seem to have regarded sanctification as brought about by a physical cleansing in which man was passive; or to have gone over to the opposite extreme, and regarded sanctification as consisting in the formation of habits of obedience. The Old School have seemed to be waiting for a physical sanctification, in which they are to be in a great measure passive, and which they have not expected to take place in this life. Holding, as they do that the constitution of both soul and body is defiled or sinful in every power and faculty, they of course cannot hold to entire sanctification in this life. If the constitutional appetites, passions, and propensities are in fact, as they hold, sinful in themselves, why then the question is settled that entire sanctification can not take place in this world nor in the next, except as the constitution is radicaly changed,

and that of course by the creative power
of God. The New School, rejecting the
doctrine of constitutional and moral depravity and physical regeneration and
sanctification,.and losing sight of Christ
as our sanctification, have fallen into a
self-righteous view of sanctification, and
have held that sanctification is effected
by works or by forming holy habits, etc.
Both the Old and New School have fallen
into egregious errors upon this fundamen-
tally important subject.

The truth is, beyond all question, that
sanctification is by faith as opposed to
works. That is, faith receives Christ in
all his offices and in all the fullness of his
relations to the soul; and Christ, when received, works in the soul to will and to do
of his good pleasure, not by a physical,
but by a moral and persuasive working.
Observe, He influences the will. This
must be by a moral influence, if its actings
are intelligent and free, as they must be
to be holy. That is, if He influences the

will to obey God, it must be by a divine moral suasion. The soul never in any instance obeys in a spiritual and true sense, except it be thus influenced by the indwelling Spirit of Christ. But whenever Christ is apprehended and received in any relation, in that relation He is full and perfect; so that we are complete in Him. For it hath pleased the Father that in Him should all fullness dwell; and that we might all receive of his fullness until we have grown up into Him in all things, "Until we all come in the unity of the faith and of the knowledge of the Son of God unto a perfect man, unto the measure of the stature of the fullness of Christ."

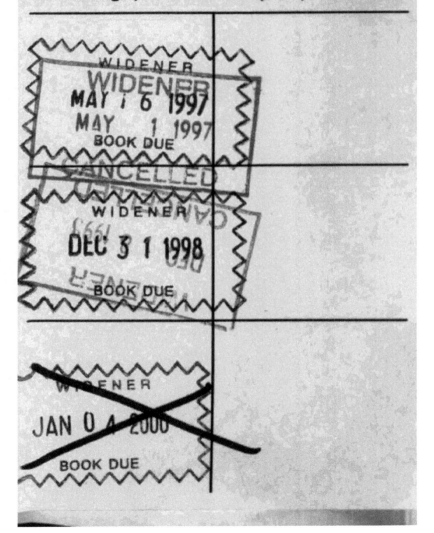

Lightning Source UK Ltd.
Milton Keynes UK
UKHW021853190721
387437UK00003B/295